U. S. and World Map Outlines

Illustrator: Mapping Specialists
Designer/Production: Moonhee Pak/Theo Dejournette
Cover Designer: Barbara Peterson
Art Director: Tom Cochrane
Project Director: Carolea Williams

Table of Contents

Countries of the World

AS = Asia
EU = Europe
AF = Africa
AU = Oceania
SA = South America
NA = North America

A

Afghanistan (Kabul) AS
Albania (Tirane) EU
Algeria (Algiers) AF
Andorra (Andorra la Vella) EU
Angola (Luanda) AF
Argentina (Buenos Aires) SA
Armenia (Yerevan) EU
Austria (Vienna) EU
Azerbaijan (Baku) AS

B

Bahamas (Nassau) NA
Bahrain (Manama) AS
Bangladesh (Dhaka) AS
Barbados (Bridgetown) NA
Belarus (Minsk) EU
Belgium (Brussels) EU
Belize (Belmopan) NA
Benin (Port-Novo) AF
Bhutan (Thimphu) AS
Bolivia (Sucre) SA
Bosnia-Herzegovina (Sarajevo) EU
Botswana (Gaborone) AF
Brazil (Brasilia) SA
Brunei (Bander Seri Begawan) AS
Bulgaria (Sofia) EU
Burkina Faso (Ouagadougou) AF
Burundi (Bujumbura) AF

C

Cambodia (Phnom Penh) AS
Cameroon (Yaounde) AF
Canada (Ottawa) NA
Cape Verde Islands (Praia) EU
Central African Republic (Bangui) AF
Chad (N'Djamena) AF
Chile (Santiago) SA
China (Beijing) AS
Colombia (Bogota) SA
Comoros (Moroni) AF

Congo (Brazzaville) AF
Congo, Democratic Republic of (Kinshasa) AF
Corsica (Bastia) EU
Costa Rica (San Jose) NA
Croatia (Zagreb) EU
Cuba (Havana) NA
Cyprus (Nicosia) AS and/or EU
Czech Republic (Prague) EU

D

Denmark (Copenhagen) EU
Djibouti (Djibouti) AF
Dominica (Roseau) NA
Dominican Republic (Santo Domingo) NA

E

East Timor (Dill) AS
Ecuador (Quito) SA
Egypt (Cairo) AF
El Salvador (San Salvador) NA
Equatorial Guinea (Malabo) AF
Eritrea (Asmara) AF
Estonia (Tallinn) EU
Ethiopia (Addis Ababa) AF

F

Falkland Islands (Stanley) EU
Figi (Suva) AU
Finland (Helsinki) EU
France (Paris) EU
French Guiana (Cayenne) SA

G

Gabon (Liberville) AF
Gambia (Banjul) AF
Georgia (Tbilisi) EU
Germany (Berlin) EU
Ghana (Accra) AF
Greece (Athens) EU
Grenada (St. George's) NA
Greenland (Nuuk) EU
Guatemala (Guatemala City) NA
Guinea (Conakry) AF
Guinea–Bissau (Bissau) AF
Guyana (Georgetown) SA

U.S. and World Map Outlines © 2004 Creative Teaching Press

H

Haiti (Port-au-Prince) AU
Honduras (Tegucigalpa) NA
Hungary (Budapest) EU

I

Iceland (Reykjavik) EU
India (New Delhi) AS
Indonesia (Jakarta) AS
Iran (Tehran) AS
Iraq (Baghdad) AS
Ireland (Dublin) EU
Israel (Jerusalem) AS
Italy (Rome) EU
Ivory Coast (Yamoussoukro) AF

J

Jamaica (Kingston) NA
Japan (Tokyo) AS
Jordan (Amman) AS

K

Kazakhstan (Astana) AS
Kenya (Nairobi) AF
Kiribati (Bairiki) AU
Korea, North (Pyongyang) AS
Korea, South (Seoul) AS
Kuwait (Kuwait City) AS
Kyrgyzstan (Bishkek) AS

L

Laos (Vientiane) AS
Latvia (Riga) EU
Lebanon (Beirut) AS
Lesotho (Maseru) AF
Liberia (Monrovia) AF
Libya (Tripoli) AF
Liechtenstein (Vaduz) EU
Lithuania (Vilnius) EU
Luxembourg (Luxembourg) EU

M

Macedonia (Skopje) EU
Madagascar (Antananarivo) AF
Malawi (Lilongwe) AF
Malaysia (Kuala Lumpur) AS
Maldives (Male) AS

Mali (Bamako) AF
Malta (Valletta) EU
Marshall Islands (Majuro) AU
Mauritania (Nouakchott) AF
Mauritius (Port Louis) AF
Mexico (Mexico City) NA
Micronesia (Palikir) AU
Moldova (Chisinau) EU
Monaco (Monaco) EU
Mongolia (Ulan Bator) AS
Morocco (Rabat) AF
Mozambique (Maputo) AF
Myanmar (Yangon) AS

N

Namibia (Windhoek) AF
Nauru (no official capital) AU
Nepal (Kathmandu) AS
Netherlands (Amsterdam) EU
Nicaragua (Managua) NA
Niger (Niamey) AF
Nigeria (Abuja) AF
Norway (Oslo) EU

O

Oman (Muscat) AS

P

Pakistan (Islamabad) AS
Palau (Koror) AU
Panama (Panama City) NA
Papua New Guinea (Port Moresby) AU
Paraguay (Asuncion) SA
Peru (Lima) SA
Philippines (Manila) AS
Poland (Warsaw) EU
Portugal (Lisbon) EU
Puerto Rico (San Juan) NA

Q

Qatar (Doha) AS

R

Romania (Bucharest) EU
Russian Federation, east of the
    Ural Mountains AS
Russian Federation, west of the Ural Mountains EU
Rwanda (Kigali) AF

S

Saint Kitts and Nevis (Basseterre) NA
Saint Lucia (Castries) NA
Saint Vincent and the Grenadines
    (Kingstown) NA
Samoa (Apia) AU
San Marino (San Marino) EU
São Tomé & Principe (Sao Tome) AF
Sardinia (Cagliari) EA
Saudi Arabia (Riyadh) AS
Senegal (Dakar) AF
Serbia-Montenegro (Belgrade) EU
Seychelles (Victoria) AF
Sicily (Palermo) EU
Sierra Leone (Freetown) AF
Singapore (Singapore City) AS
Slovakia (Bratislava) EU
Slovenia (Ljubljana) EU
Soloman Islands (Honiara) AU
Somalia (Mogadishu) AF
South Africa (Pretoria, Cape Town,
    Bloemfontein) AF
Spain (Madrid) EU
Sri Lanka (Colombo) AS
Sudan (Khartoum) AF
Suriname (Paramaribo) SA
Swaziland (Mbabane) AF
Sweden (Stockholm) EU
Switzerland (Bern) EU
Syria (Damascus) AS

T

Taiwan (Taipei) AS
Tajikistan (Dushanbe) AS
Tanzania (Dodoma) AF
Thailand (Bangkok) AS
Togo (Lome) AF
Tonga (Nuku'alofa) AU
Trinidad and Tobago (Port-of-Spain) NA
Tunisia (Tunis) AF
Turkey (Ankara) AS and EU
Turkmenistan (Ashgabat) AS
Tuvalu (Funafuti) AU

U

Uganda (Kampala) AF
Ukraine (Kiev) EU
United Arab Emirates (Abu Dhabi) AS
United Kingdom (England, Wales, Northern
    Ireland, Scotland) (London) EU
United States (Washington, D.C.) NA
Uruguay (Montevideo) SA
Uzbekistan (Tashkent) AS

V

Vanuatu (Port-Vila) AU
Vatican City EU
Venezuela (Caracas) SA
Vietnam (Hanoi) AS

W

Western Sahara AF

Y

Yemen (Sana) AS

Z

Zambia (Lusaka) AF
Zimbabwe (Harare) AF

U.S. and World Map Outlines © 2004 Creative Teaching Press

Top Ten Lists

Ten Largest Countries

1. Russia   17,075,400 sq. km. (6,592,846 sq. miles)
2. Canada   9,330,970 sq. km. (3,602,707 sq. miles)
3. China   9,326,410 sq. km. (3,600,947 sq. miles)
4. United States   9,166,600 sq. km. (3,539,242 sq. miles)
5. Brazil   8,456,510 sq. km. (3,265,075 sq. miles)
6. Australia   7,617,930 sq. km. (2,941,283 sq. miles)
7. India   2,973,190 sq. km. (1,147,949 sq. miles)
8. Argentina   2,736,690 sq. km. (1,056,636 sq. miles)
9. Kazakhstan   2,717,300 sq. km. (1,049,150 sq. miles)
10. Sudan   2,376,000 sq. km. (917,374 sq. miles)

Ten Largest United States Cities (by population)

1. New York City, NY   8.04 million
2. Los Angeles, CA   3.7 million
3. Chicago, IL   2.9 million
4. Houston, TX   2.05 million
5. Philadelphia, PA   1.61 million
6. Phoenix, AZ   1.39 million
7. San Antonio, TX   1.36 million
8. San Diego, CA   1.3 million
9. Dallas, TX   1.25 million
10. Detroit, MI   1.1 million

Ten Tallest Mountains

1. Mount Everest   8,850 m (29,035 ft) Nepal
2. Qogir (K2)   8,611 m (28,250 ft) Pakistan
3. Kangchenjunga   8,586 m (28,169 ft) Nepal
4. Lhotse   8,501 m (27,920 ft) Nepal
5. Makalu I   8,462 m (27,765 ft) Nepal
6. Cho Oyu   8,201 m (26,906 ft) Nepal
7. Dhaulagiri   8,167 m (26,794 ft) Nepal
8. Manaslu I   8,156 m (26,758 ft) Nepal
9. Nanga Parbat   8,125 m (26,658 ft) Pakistan
10. Annapurna I   8,091 m (26,545 ft) Nepal

Ten Most Common Languages

1. Chinese Mandarin   1 billion +
2. English   512 million
3. Hindustania   498 million
4. Spanish   391 million
5. Russian   280 million
6. Arabic   245 million
7. Bengali   211 million
8. Portuguese   192 million
9. Malay-Indonesian   160 million
10. Japanese   125 million

Ten Longest Rivers

1. Nile, Africa   6,825 km
2. Amazon, South America   6,437 km
3. Chang Jiang (Yangtze), Asia   6,380 km
4. Mississippi, North America   5,971 km
5. Yenisey-Angara, Asia   5,536 km
6. Huang (Yellow), Asia   5,464 km
7. Ob-Irtysh, Asia   5,410 km
8. Amur, Asia   4,416 km
9. Lena, Asia   4,400 km
10. Congo, Africa   4,370 km

Ten Largest Metropolitan Areas of the World (by population)

1. Toyko, Japan   31.4 million
2. New York City/Philadelphia, USA 30.05 million
3. Mexico City, Mexico   20.98 million
4. Seoul, South Korea   19.85 million
5. Sao Paulo, Brazil   18.5 million
6. Osaka-Kobe-Kyoto, Japan   17.6 million
7. Jakarta, Indonesia   17.58 million
8. New Delhi, India   16.7 million
9. Mumbai, India (Bombay)   16.69 million
10. Los Angeles, USA   16.62 million

World Map

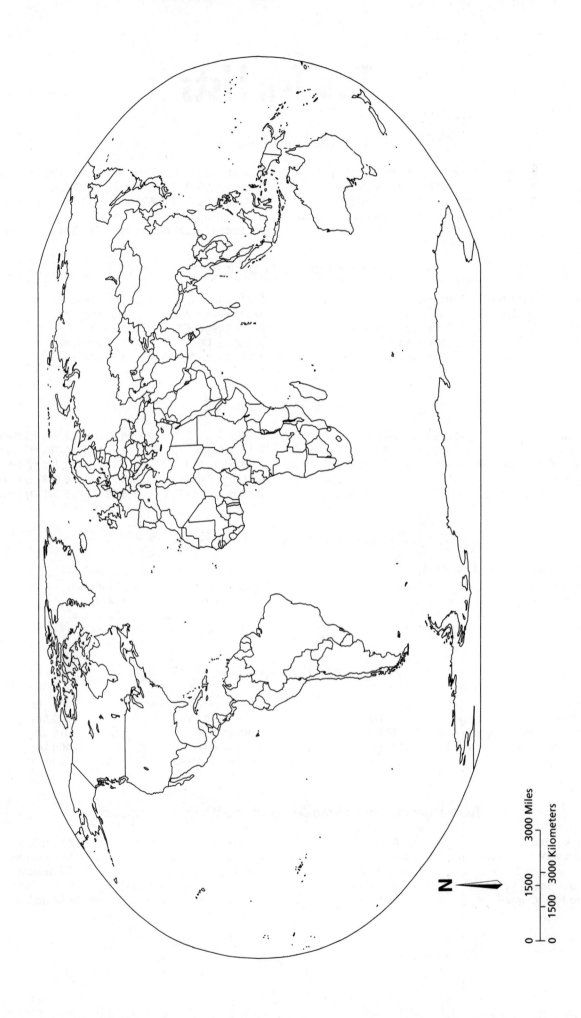

N

3000 Miles

3000 Kilometers

0   1500

0   1500

World Map

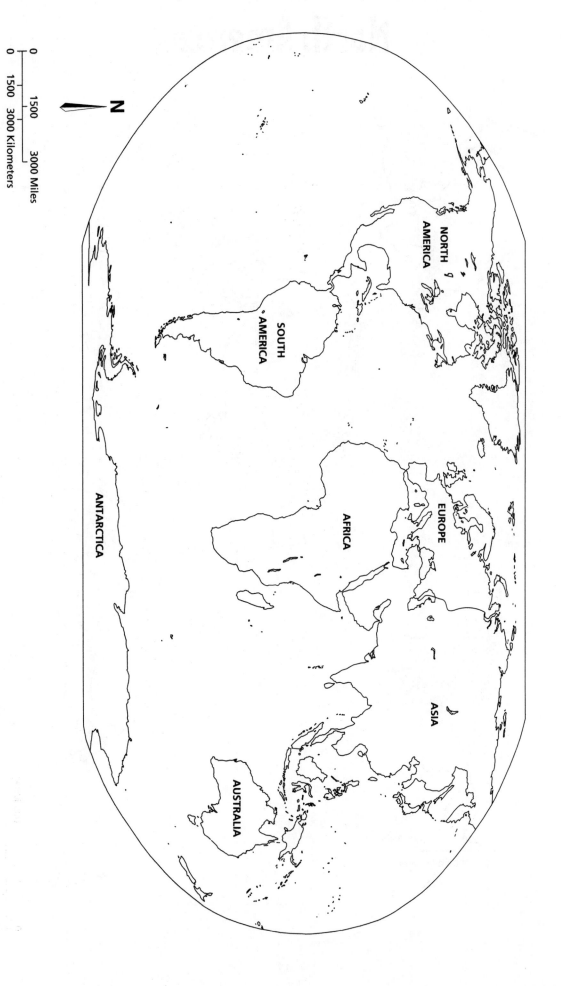

ANTARCTICA

NORTH AMERICA

SOUTH AMERICA

EUROPE

AFRICA

ASIA

AUSTRALIA

N

0   1500   3000 Miles
0   1500   3000 Kilometers

North America

N

| 0 | 500 | 1000 Miles |

| 0 | 500 | 1000 Kilometers |

U.S. and World Map Outlines © 2004 Creative Teaching Press

North America

Alaska
(U.S.)

CANADA

UNITED STATES

MEXICO

BAHAMAS

DOMINICAN
REPUBLIC

CUBA

JAMAICA

HAITI

BELIZE

HONDURAS

NICARAGUA

GUATEMALA

PANAMA

EL SALVADOR

COSTA RICA

N

0	500	1000 Miles

0	500	1000 Kilometers

South America

N

| 0 | | 400 | | 800 Miles |
| 0 | 400 | | 800 Kilometers | |

South America

TRINIDAD
AND TOBAGO

SURINAME

FRENCH
GUIANA
(Fr.)

VENEZUELA

GUYANA

COLOMBIA

ECUADOR

BRAZIL

PERU

BOLIVIA

PARAGUAY

CHILE

ARGENTINA

URUGUAY

N

FALKLAND IS.
(U.K.)

0   400   800 Miles

0   400   800 Kilometers

Africa

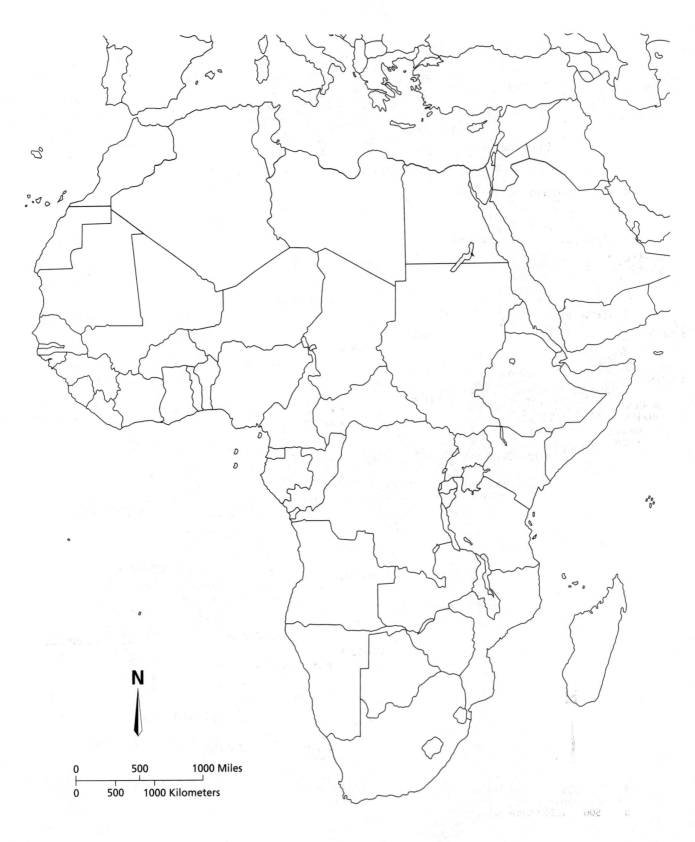

N

| 0 | 500 | 1000 Miles |

| 0 | 500 | 1000 Kilometers |

Africa

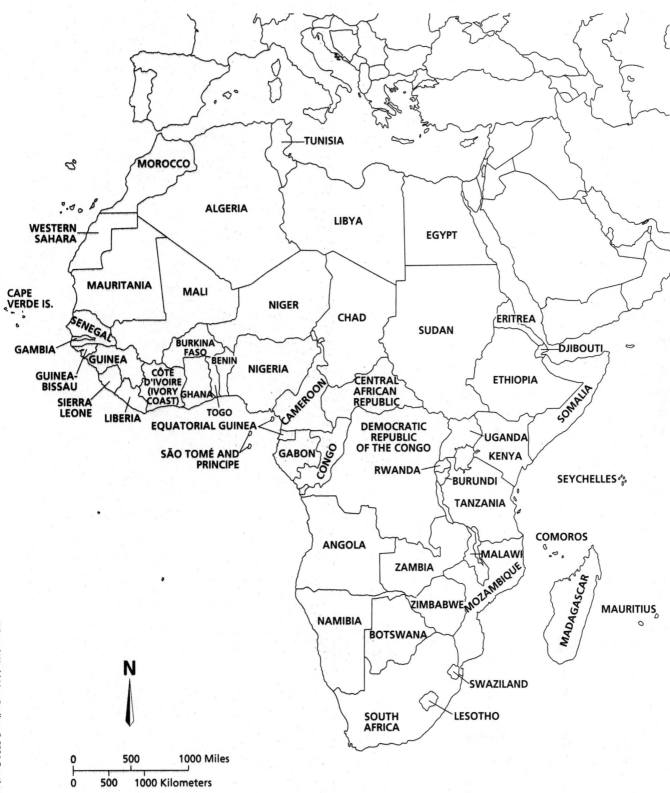

TUNISIA

MOROCCO

ALGERIA

LIBYA

EGYPT

WESTERN SAHARA

CAPE VERDE IS.

MAURITANIA

MALI

NIGER

CHAD

SUDAN

ERITREA

DJIBOUTI

SENEGAL

GAMBIA

GUINEA

BURKINA FASO

BENIN

NIGERIA

CENTRAL AFRICAN REPUBLIC

ETHIOPIA

SOMALIA

GUINEA-BISSAU

CÔTE D'IVOIRE (IVORY COAST)

GHANA

TOGO

CAMEROON

SIERRA LEONE

LIBERIA

EQUATORIAL GUINEA

DEMOCRATIC REPUBLIC OF THE CONGO

UGANDA

KENYA

SÃO TOMÉ AND PRINCIPE

GABON

CONGO

RWANDA

BURUNDI

SEYCHELLES

TANZANIA

COMOROS

ANGOLA

ZAMBIA

MALAWI

NAMIBIA

ZIMBABWE

MOZAMBIQUE

MADAGASCAR

MAURITIUS

BOTSWANA

SWAZILAND

SOUTH AFRICA

LESOTHO

N

0	500	1000 Miles

0	500	1000 Kilometers

Europe

N

| 0 | 300 | 600 Miles |

| 0 | 300 | 600 Kilometers |

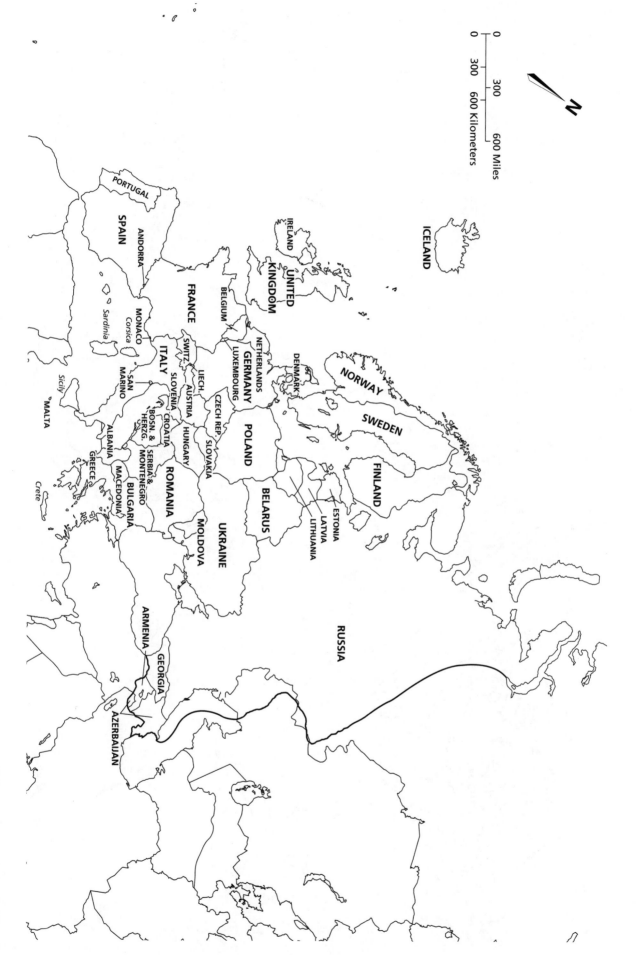

Europe

PORTUGAL
SPAIN
ANDORRA
IRELAND
UNITED KINGDOM
ICELAND
FRANCE
BELGIUM
NETHERLANDS
DENMARK
NORWAY
SWEDEN
Sardinia
Corsica
MONACO
SWITZ.
ITALY
SAN MARINO
GERMANY
LUXEMBOURG
LIECH.
SLOVENIA
AUSTRIA
CZECH REP.
POLAND
FINLAND
Sicily
MALTA
ALBANIA
GREECE
Crete
MACEDONIA
BULGARIA
ROMANIA
BOSN. & HERZG.
CROATIA
SERBIA & MONTENEGRO
HUNGARY
SLOVAKIA
MOLDOVA
UKRAINE
BELARUS
ESTONIA
LATVIA
LITHUANIA
RUSSIA
ARMENIA
GEORGIA
AZERBAIJAN

0
300
600 Kilometers
0
300
600 Miles

N

Asia

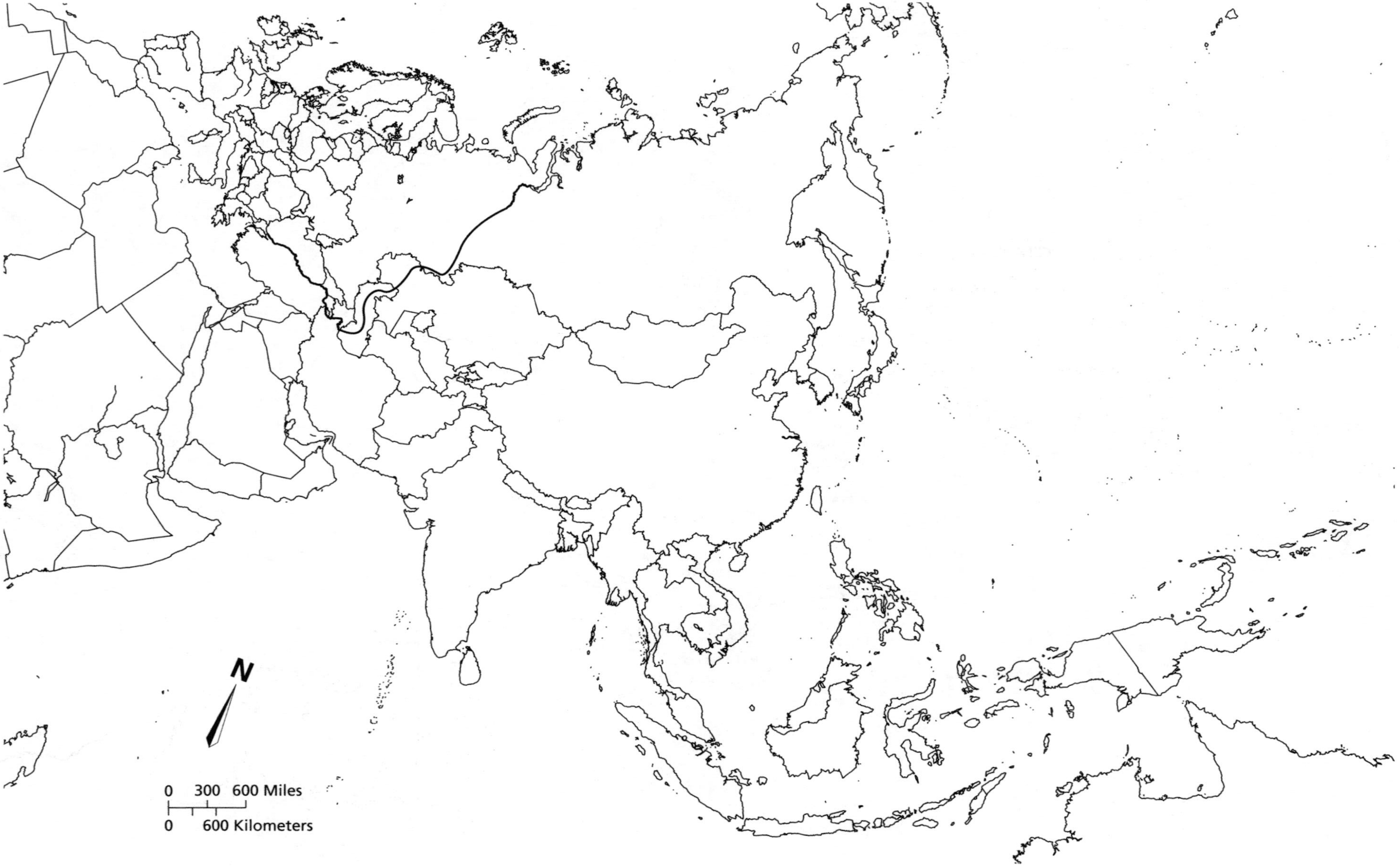

U.S. and World Map Outlines © 2004 Creative Teaching Press

N

300 600 Miles

0

600 Kilometers

0

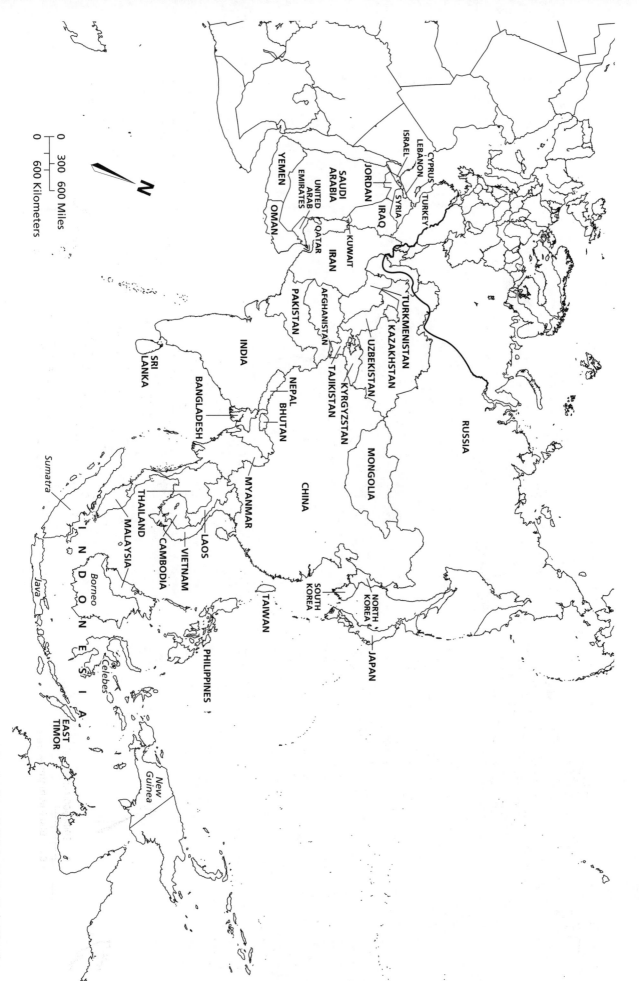

Asia

SRI LANKA

INDIA

PAKISTAN

AFGHANISTAN

IRAN

IRAQ

KUWAIT

QATAR

UNITED ARAB EMIRATES

OMAN

SAUDI ARABIA

YEMEN

JORDAN

SYRIA

ISRAEL

LEBANON

CYPRUS

TURKEY

TURKMENISTAN

UZBEKISTAN

KAZAKHSTAN

TAJIKISTAN

KYRGYZSTAN

MONGOLIA

RUSSIA

NEPAL

BHUTAN

BANGLADESH

MYANMAR

CHINA

THAILAND

LAOS

VIETNAM

CAMBODIA

MALAYSIA

TAIWAN

SOUTH KOREA

NORTH KOREA

JAPAN

PHILIPPINES

Sumatra

Java

Borneo

Celebes

EAST TIMOR

New Guinea

INDONESIA

N

0   300   600 Miles

0   600 Kilometers

Australia

N

| 0 | 500 | | 500 | 1000 Kilometers | |
| 0 | | 500 | | 1000 Miles | |

Australia Territories

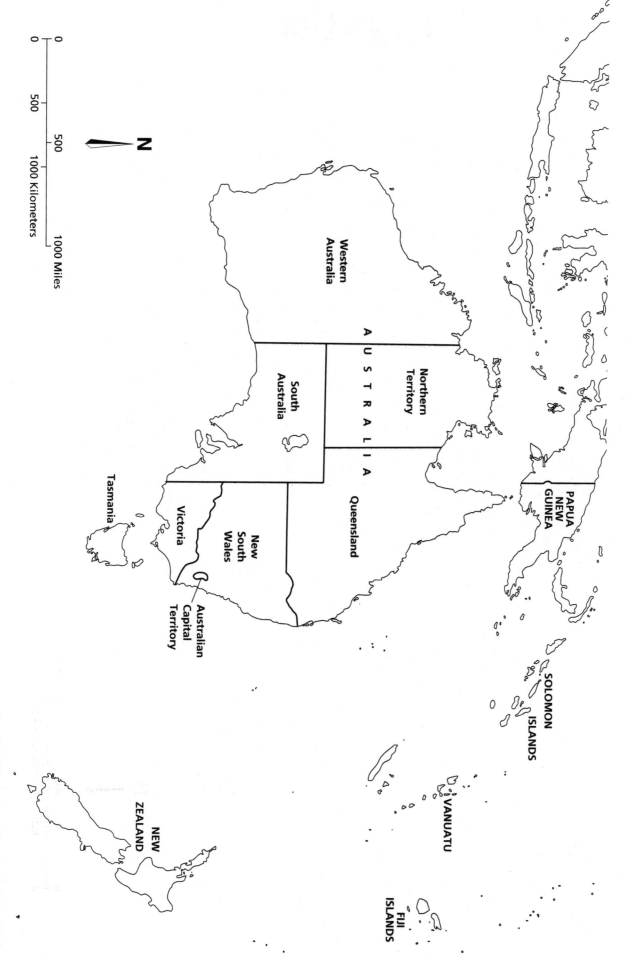

N

0
500
500
1000 Kilometers
1000 Miles

Western
Australia

A U S T R A L I A

Northern
Territory

South
Australia

Queensland

Tasmania

Victoria

New
South
Wales

Australian
Capital
Territory

PAPUA
NEW
GUINEA

SOLOMON
ISLANDS

VANUATU

FIJI
ISLANDS

NEW
ZEALAND

Antarctica

A N T A R C T I C A

+ SOUTH POLE

N

| 0 | 300 | 600 Miles |
| 0 | 300 | 600 Kilometers |

Northern Africa

WESTERN SAHARA, MOROCCO, ALGERIA, TUNISIA

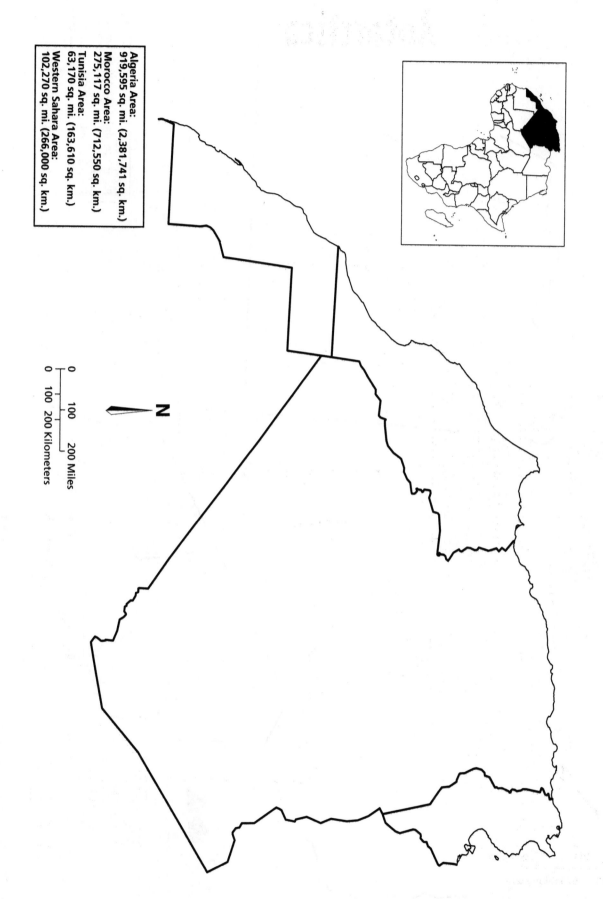

Algeria Area:
919,595 sq. mi. (2,381,741 sq. km.)

Morocco Area:
275,117 sq. mi. (712,550 sq. km.)

Tunisia Area:
63,170 sq. mi. (163,610 sq. km.)

Western Sahara Area:
102,270 sq. mi. (266,000 sq. km.)

N

0   100   200 Miles
0   100   200 Kilometers

Northern Africa

LIBYA, EGYPT

Egypt Area:
386,662 sq. mi. (1,001,449 sq. km.)

Libya Area:
679,362 sq. mi. (1,759,540 sq. km.)

N

400 Miles

400 Kilometers

200

200

0

0

Western Africa

CAPE VERDE ISLANDS, SENEGAL, GAMBIA, GUINEA–BISSAU, GUINEA, SIERRA LEONE, LIBERIA

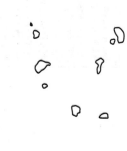

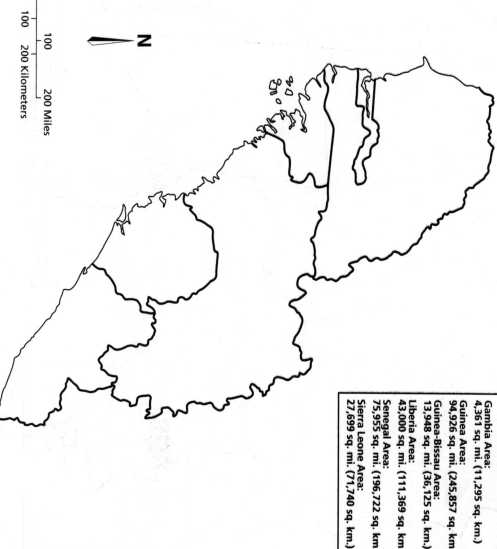

N

0   0
100   100
200   100
     200 Kilometers
     200 Miles

Cape Verde Area:
1,557 sq. mi. (4,033 sq. km.)
Gambia Area:
4,361 sq. mi. (11,295 sq. km.)
Guinea Area:
94,926 sq. mi. (245,857 sq. km.)
Guinea-Bissau Area:
13,948 sq. mi. (36,125 sq. km.)
Liberia Area:
43,000 sq. mi. (111,369 sq. km.)
Senegal Area:
75,955 sq. mi. (196,722 sq. km.)
Sierra Leone Area:
27,699 sq. mi. (71,740 sq. km.)

Western Africa

IVORY COAST, GHANA, TOGO, BENIN, BURKINA FASO

Benin Area:
43,484 sq. mi. (112,622 sq. km.)
Burkina Faso Area:
105,869 sq. mi. (274,200 sq. km.)
Ghana Area:
92,100 sq. mi. (238,537 sq. km.)
Ivory Coast Area:
124,504 sq. mi. (322,463 sq. km.)
Togo Area:
21,925 sq. mi. (56,785 sq. km.)

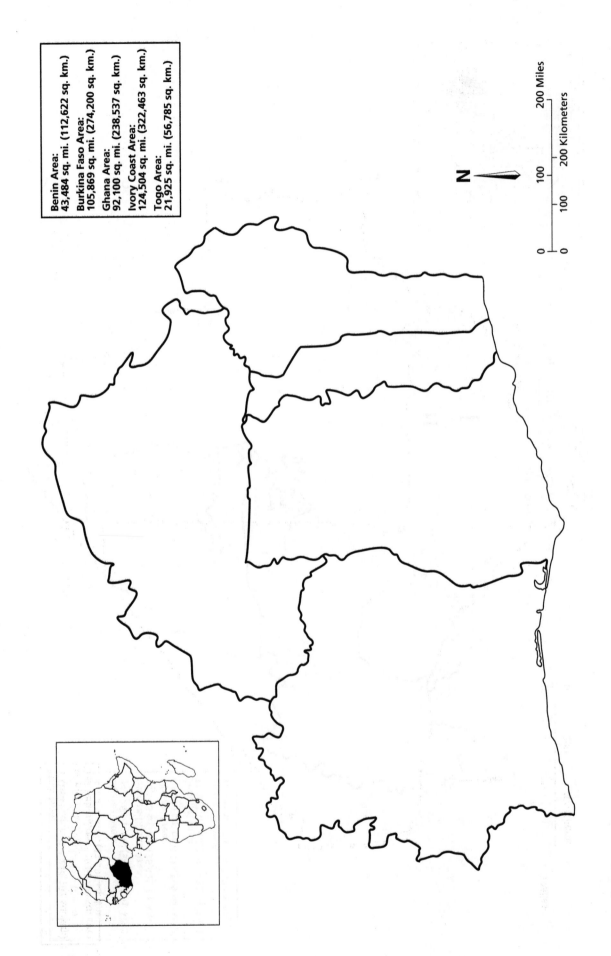

N

0	100	200 Miles
0	100	200 Kilometers

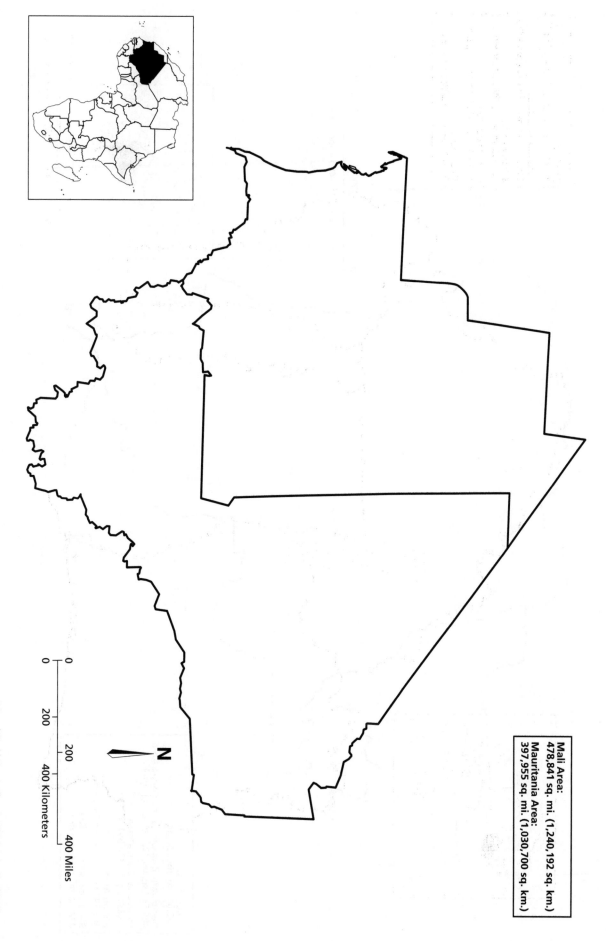

Western Africa

MAURITANIA, MALI

Mali Area:
478,841 sq. mi. (1,240,192 sq. km.)
Mauritania Area:
397,955 sq. mi. (1,030,700 sq. km.)

N

0
200
400 Kilometers

0
200
400 Miles

Western Africa

EQUATORIAL GUINEA, SÃO TOMÉ & PRINCIPE, GABON, CONGO REPUBLIC, DEMOCRATIC REPUBLIC OF THE CONGO

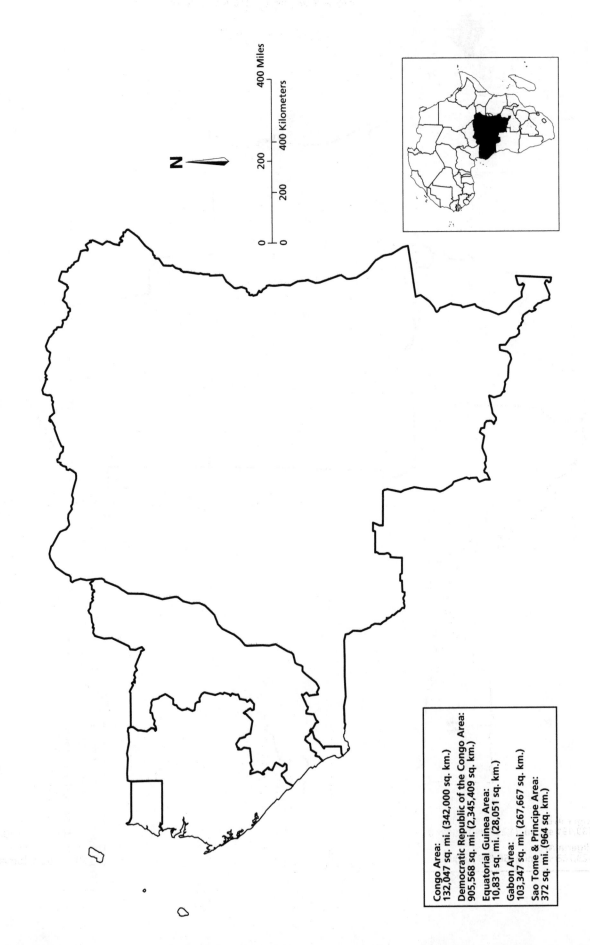

400 Miles

N

400 Kilometers

0   200   400

0   200

Congo Area:
132,047 sq. mi. (342,000 sq. km.)

Democratic Republic of the Congo Area:
905,568 sq. mi. (2,345,409 sq. km.)

Equatorial Guinea Area:
10,831 sq. mi. (28,051 sq. km.)

Gabon Area:
103,347 sq. mi. (267,667 sq. km.)

Sao Tome & Principe Area:
372 sq. mi. (964 sq. km.)

Central Africa

NIGERIA, NIGER

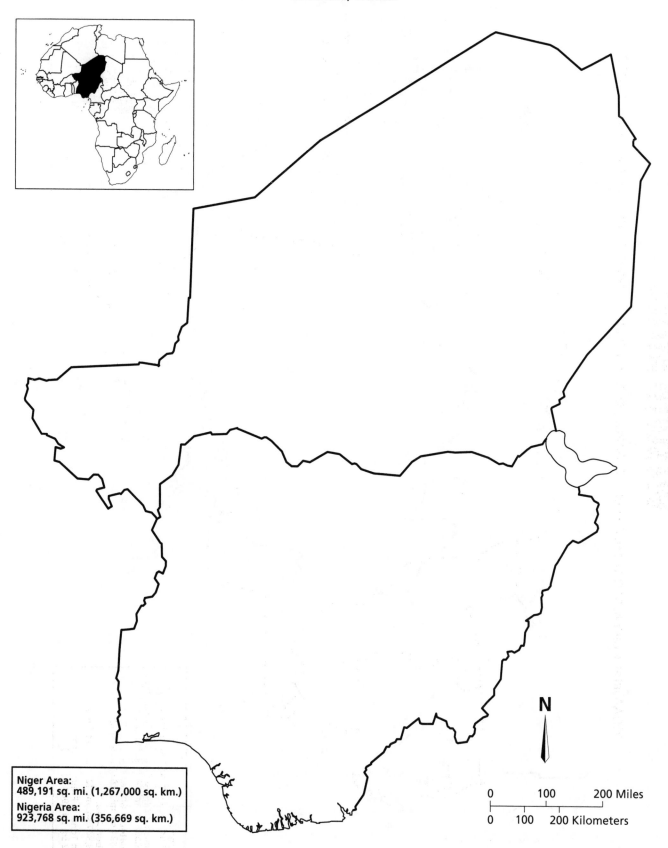

N

| 0 | 100 | 200 Miles |

| 0 | 100 | 200 Kilometers |

Niger Area:
489,191 sq. mi. (1,267,000 sq. km.)
Nigeria Area:
923,768 sq. mi. (356,669 sq. km.)

Central Africa

CAMEROON, CHAD, CENTRAL AFRICAN REPUBLIC

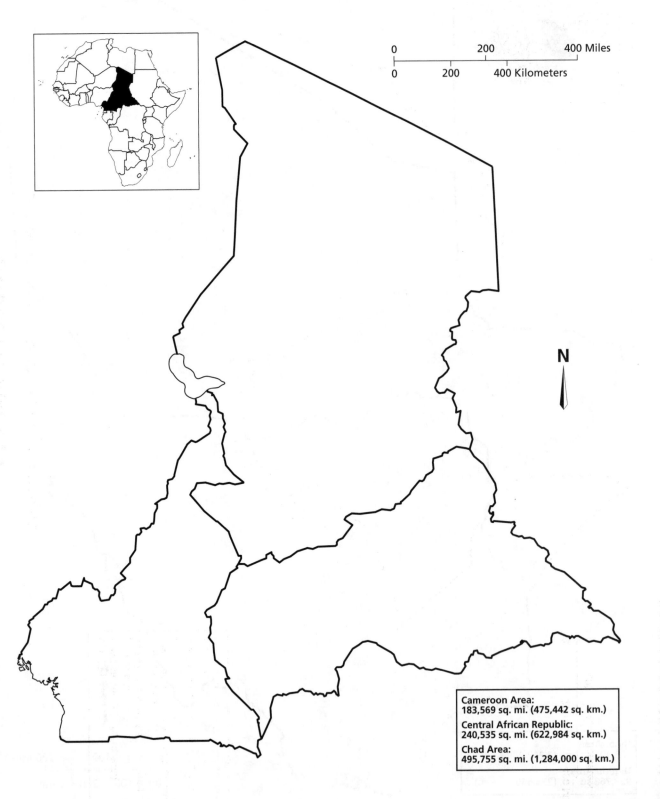

0   200   400 Miles

0   200   400 Kilometers

N

Cameroon Area:
183,569 sq. mi. (475,442 sq. km.)

Central African Republic:
240,535 sq. mi. (622,984 sq. km.)

Chad Area:
495,755 sq. mi. (1,284,000 sq. km.)

Eastern Africa

SUDAN, ERITREA, DJIBOUTI, SOMALIA, ETHIOPIA

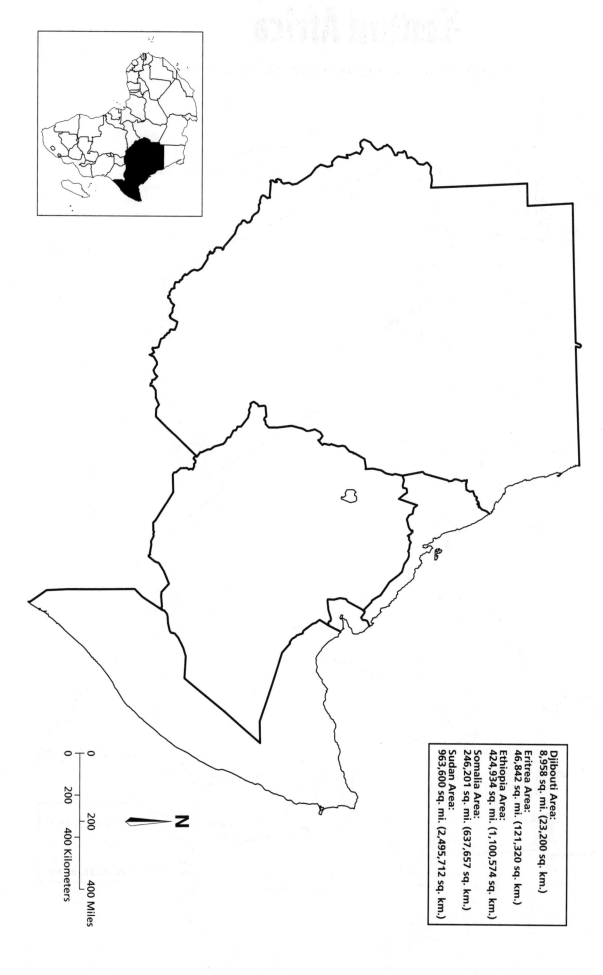

Djibouti Area:
8,958 sq. mi. (23,200 sq. km.)
Eritrea Area:
46,842 sq. mi. (121,320 sq. km.)
Ethiopia Area:
424,934 sq. mi. (1,100,574 sq. km.)
Somalia Area:
246,201 sq. mi. (637,657 sq. km.)
Sudan Area:
963,600 sq. mi. (2,495,712 sq. km.)

N

0   200   400 Miles
0   200   400 Kilometers

U.S. and World Map Outlines © 2004 Creative Teaching Press

Eastern Africa

UGANDA, KENYA, RWANDA, BURUNDI, TANZANIA

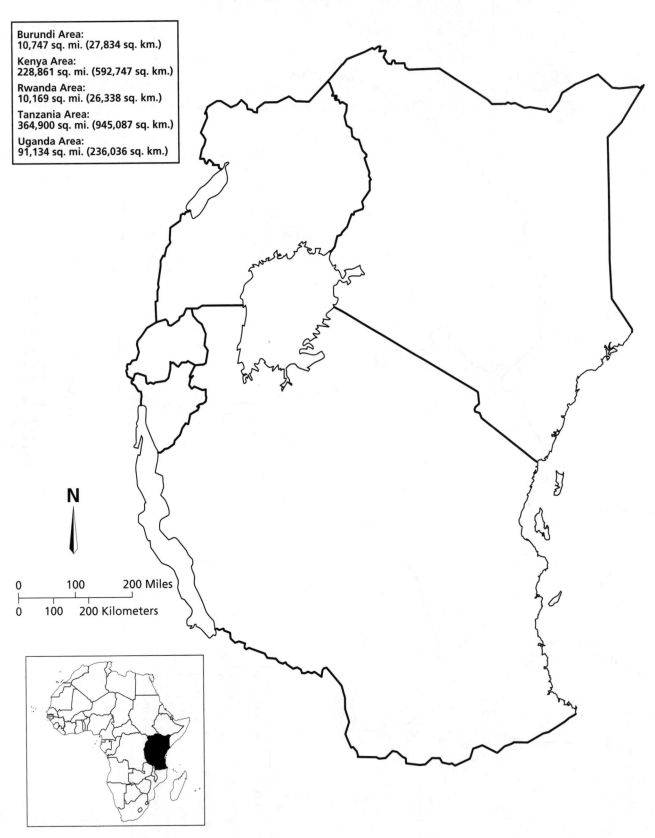

Burundi Area:
10,747 sq. mi. (27,834 sq. km.)

Kenya Area:
228,861 sq. mi. (592,747 sq. km.)

Rwanda Area:
10,169 sq. mi. (26,338 sq. km.)

Tanzania Area:
364,900 sq. mi. (945,087 sq. km.)

Uganda Area:
91,134 sq. mi. (236,036 sq. km.)

N

0   100   200 Miles
0   100   200 Kilometers

Southern Africa

ANGOLA, NAMIBIA

Angola Area:
481,354 sq. mi. (1,246,700 sq. km.)

Namibia Area:
318,261 sq. mi. (824,292 sq. km.)

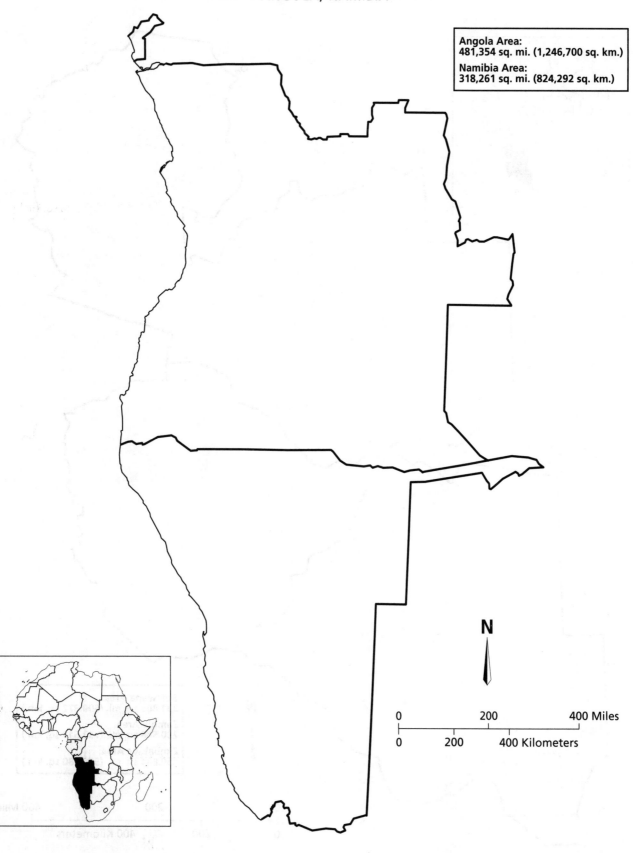

N

| 0 | | 200 | | 400 Miles |
| 0 | 200 | | 400 Kilometers | |

Southern Africa

ZAMBIA, BOTSWANA, ZIMBABWE

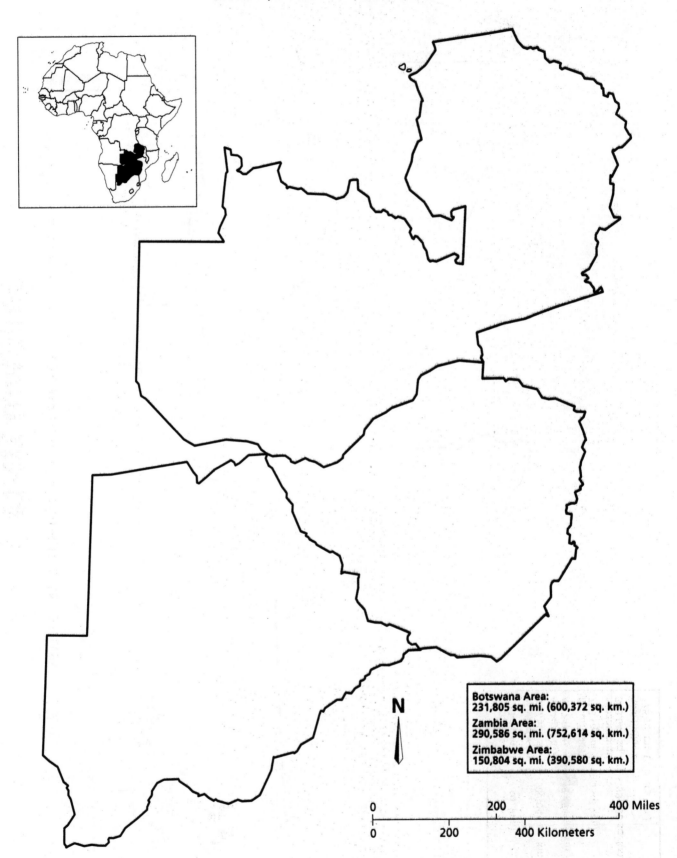

Botswana Area:
231,805 sq. mi. (600,372 sq. km.)

Zambia Area:
290,586 sq. mi. (752,614 sq. km.)

Zimbabwe Area:
150,804 sq. mi. (390,580 sq. km.)

N

| 0 | | 200 | | 400 Miles |
| 0 | 200 | | 400 Kilometers | |

U.S. and World Map Outlines © 2004 Creative Teaching Press

Southern Africa

MALAWI, MOZAMBIQUE, COMOROS, MADAGASCAR, MAURITIUS, SEYCHELLES

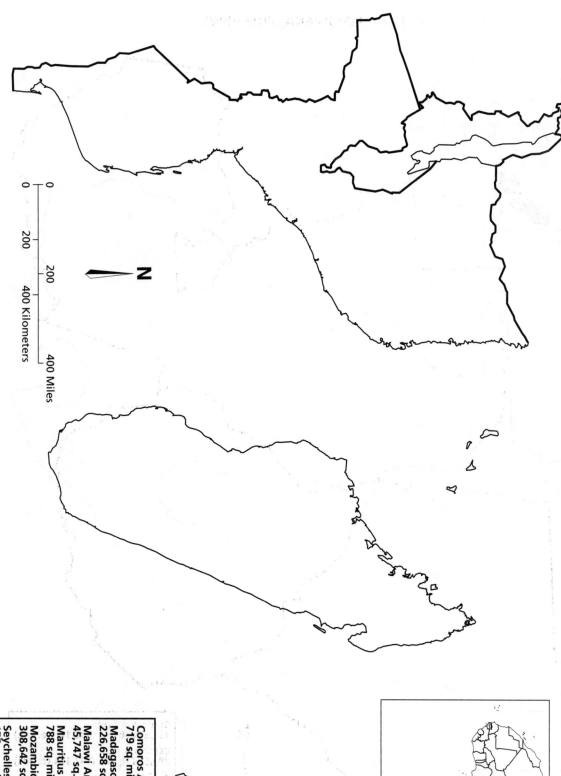

N

0
0

200

200

400 Kilometers

400 Miles

Comoros Area:
719 sq. mi. (1,862 sq. km.)

Madagascar Area:
226,658 sq. mi. (587,041 sq. km.)

Malawi Area:
45,747 sq. mi. (118,484 sq. km.)

Mauritius Area:
788 sq. mi. (2,040 sq. km.)

Mozambique Area:
308,642 sq. mi. (799,380 sq. km.)

Seychelles Area:
175 sq. mi. (453 sq. km.)

Southern Africa

SOUTH AFRICA, LESOTHO, SWAZILAND

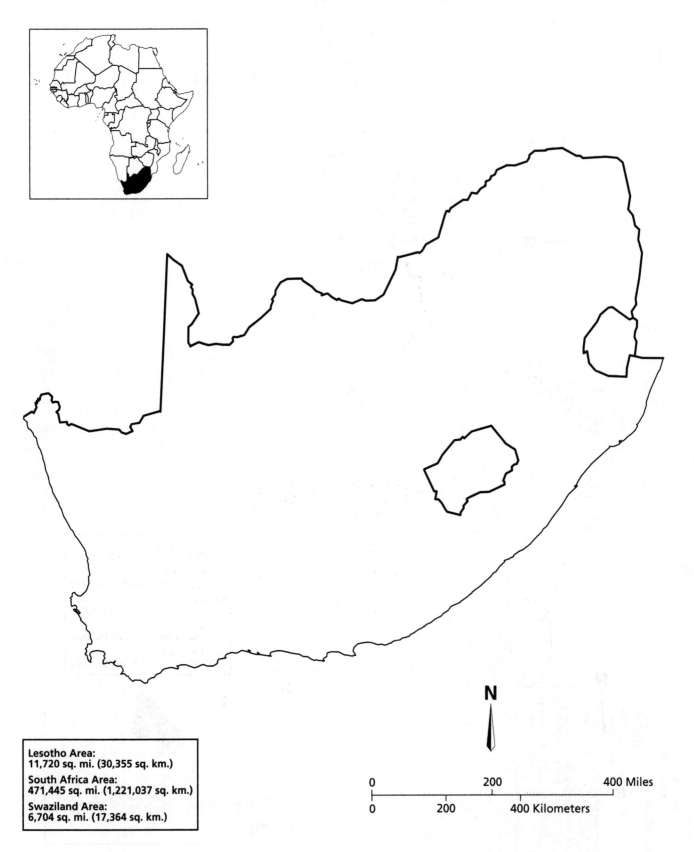

Lesotho Area:
11,720 sq. mi. (30,355 sq. km.)

South Africa Area:
471,445 sq. mi. (1,221,037 sq. km.)

Swaziland Area:
6,704 sq. mi. (17,364 sq. km.)

N

| 0 | 200 | 400 Miles |

| 0 | 200 | 400 Kilometers |

Northern Europe

NORWAY, SWEDEN, DENMARK, FINLAND, ICELAND

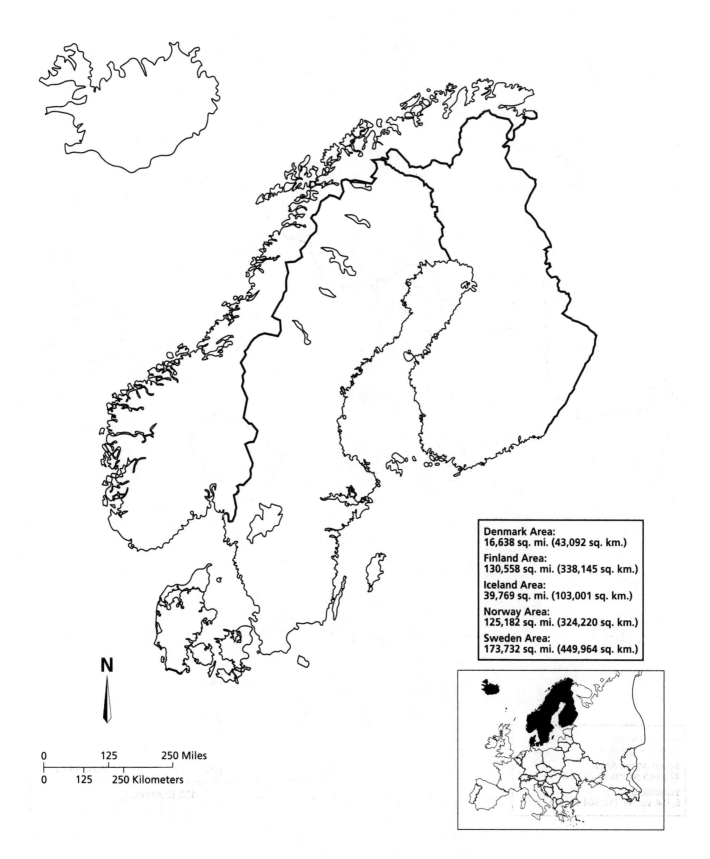

Denmark Area:
16,638 sq. mi. (43,092 sq. km.)

Finland Area:
130,558 sq. mi. (338,145 sq. km.)

Iceland Area:
39,769 sq. mi. (103,001 sq. km.)

Norway Area:
125,182 sq. mi. (324,220 sq. km.)

Sweden Area:
173,732 sq. mi. (449,964 sq. km.)

N

0	125	250 Miles
0	125	250 Kilometers

Western Europe

UNITED KINGDOM (ENGLAND, WALES, NORTHERN IRELAND, SCOTLAND), IRELAND

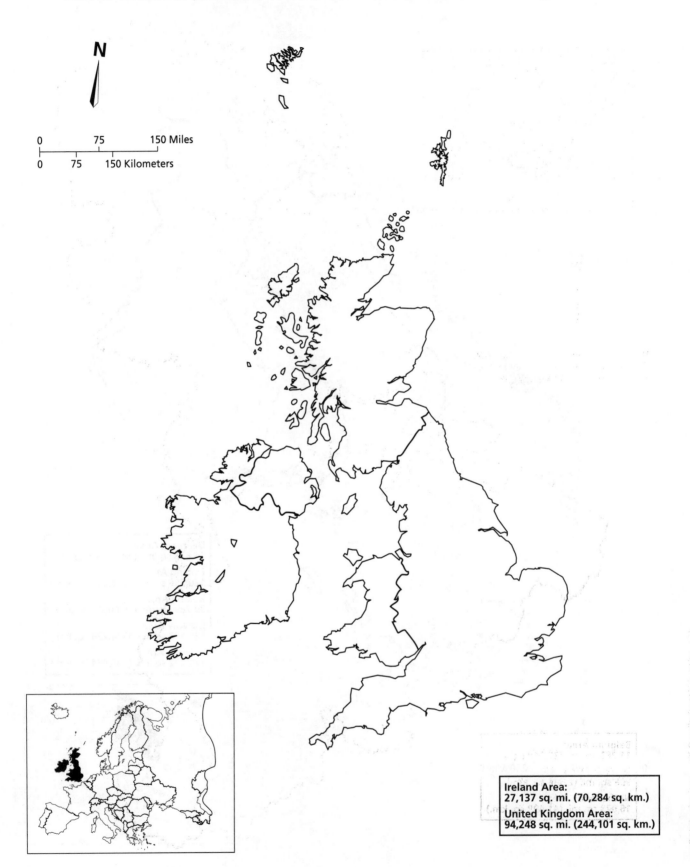

N

0   75   150 Miles
0   75   150 Kilometers

Ireland Area:
27,137 sq. mi. (70,284 sq. km.)

United Kingdom Area:
94,248 sq. mi. (244,101 sq. km.)

Western Europe

NETHERLANDS, BELGIUM, LUXEMBOURG

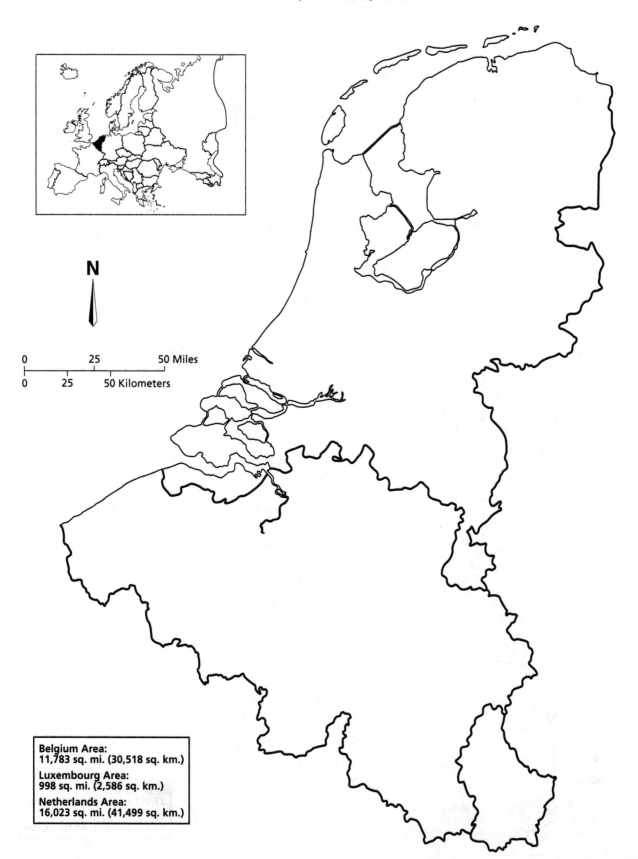

N

| 0 | 25 | 50 Miles |
| 0 | 25 | 50 Kilometers |

Belgium Area:
11,783 sq. mi. (30,518 sq. km.)

Luxembourg Area:
998 sq. mi. (2,586 sq. km.)

Netherlands Area:
16,023 sq. mi. (41,499 sq. km.)

Western Europe

FRANCE, MONACO, CORSICA

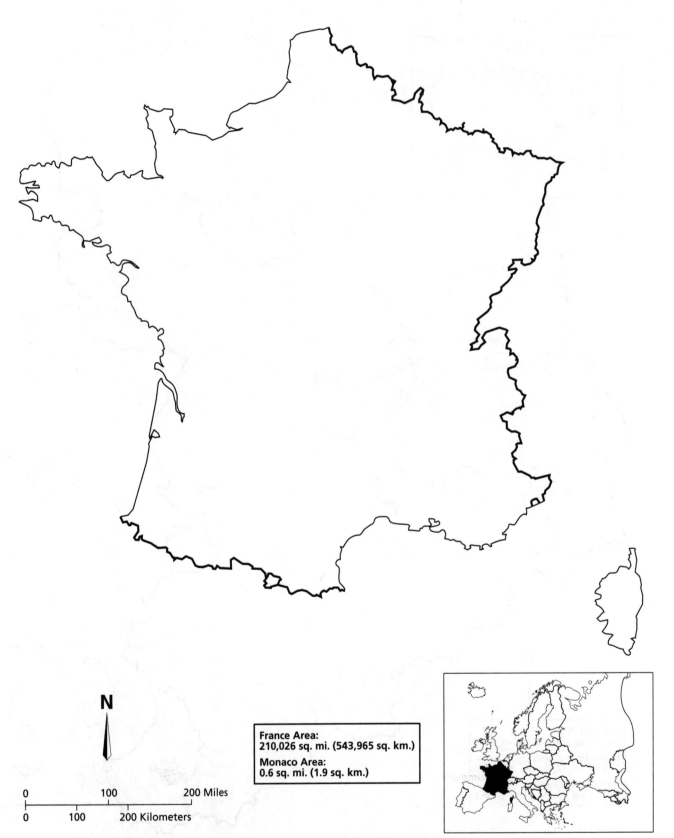

N

France Area:
210,026 sq. mi. (543,965 sq. km.)

Monaco Area:
0.6 sq. mi. (1.9 sq. km.)

0   100   200 Miles
0   100   200 Kilometers

Southwestern Europe

SPAIN, PORTUGAL, ANDORRA

Andorra Area:
175 sq. mi. (453 sq. km.)

Portugal Area:
35,672 sq. mi. (92,389 sq. km.)

Spain Area:
194,897 sq. mi. (504,782 sq. km.)

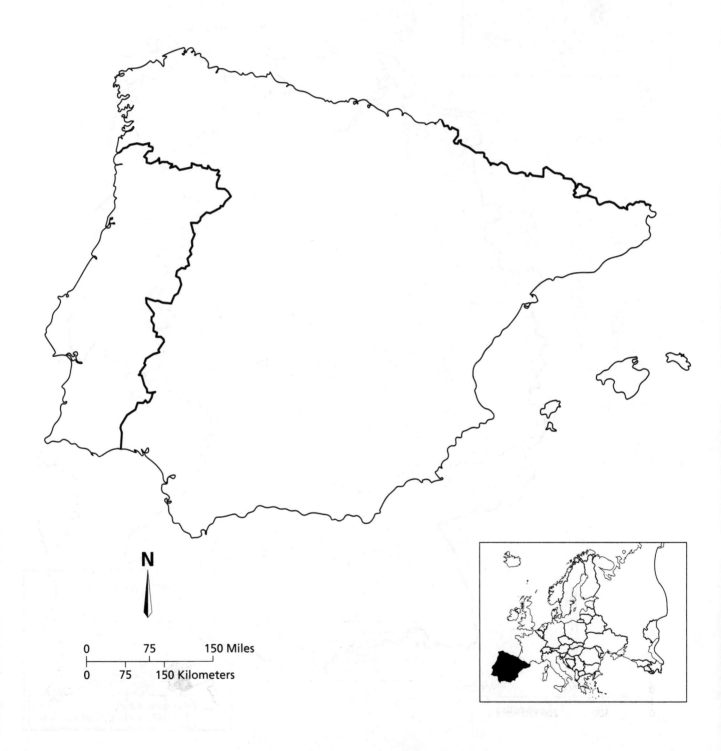

N

| 0 | 75 | 150 Miles |
| 0 | 75 | 150 Kilometers |

Central Europe

GERMANY

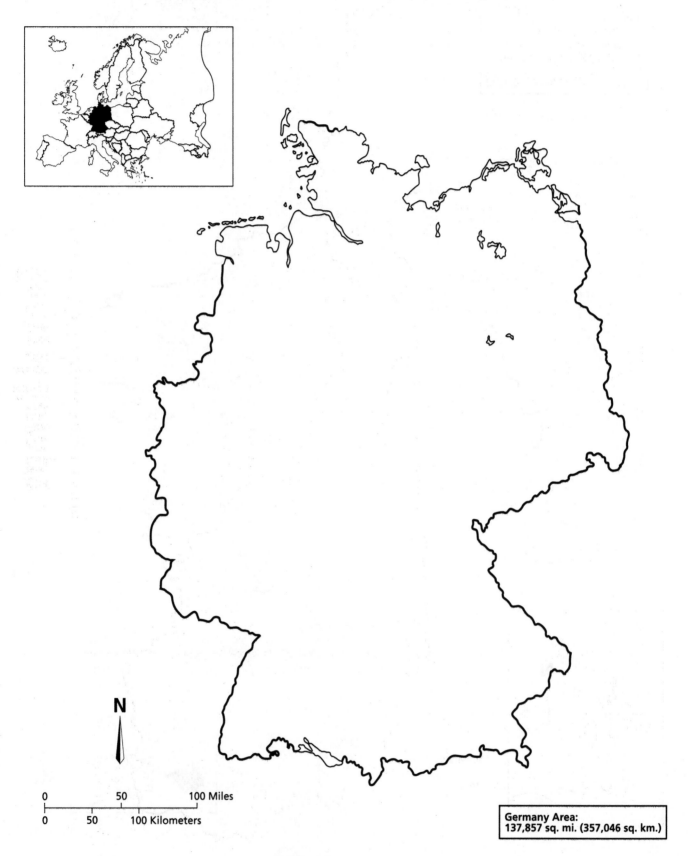

N

| 0 | 50 | 100 Miles |
| 0 | 50 | 100 Kilometers |

Germany Area:
137,857 sq. mi. (357,046 sq. km.)

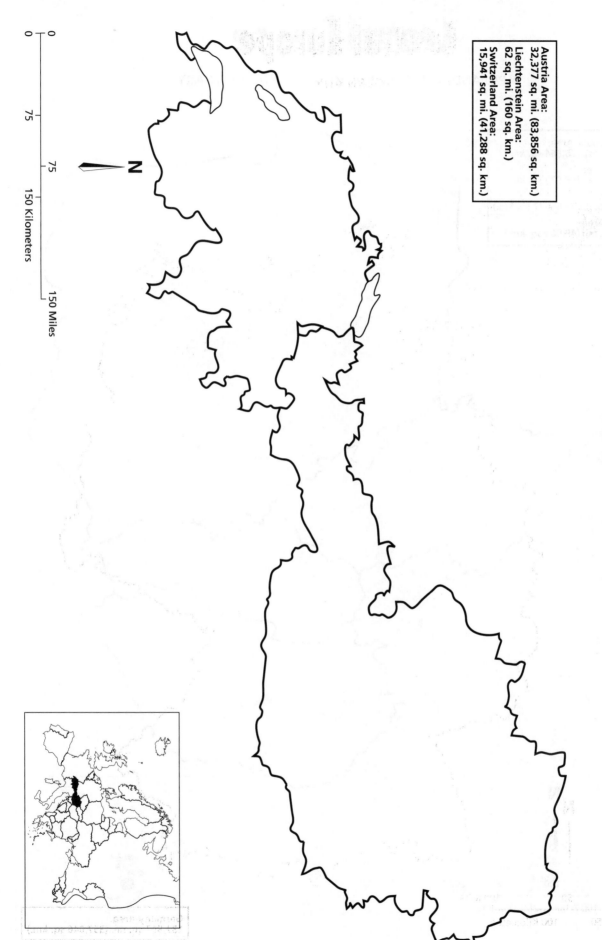

Central Europe

SWITZERLAND, AUSTRIA, LIECHTENSTEIN

Austria Area:
32,377 sq. mi. (83,856 sq. km.)
Liechtenstein Area:
62 sq. mi. (160 sq. km.)
Switzerland Area:
15,941 sq. mi. (41,288 sq. km.)

N

0

75

75

150 Kilometers

150 Miles

Central Europe

POLAND, CZECH REPUBLIC, SLOVAKIA, HUNGARY

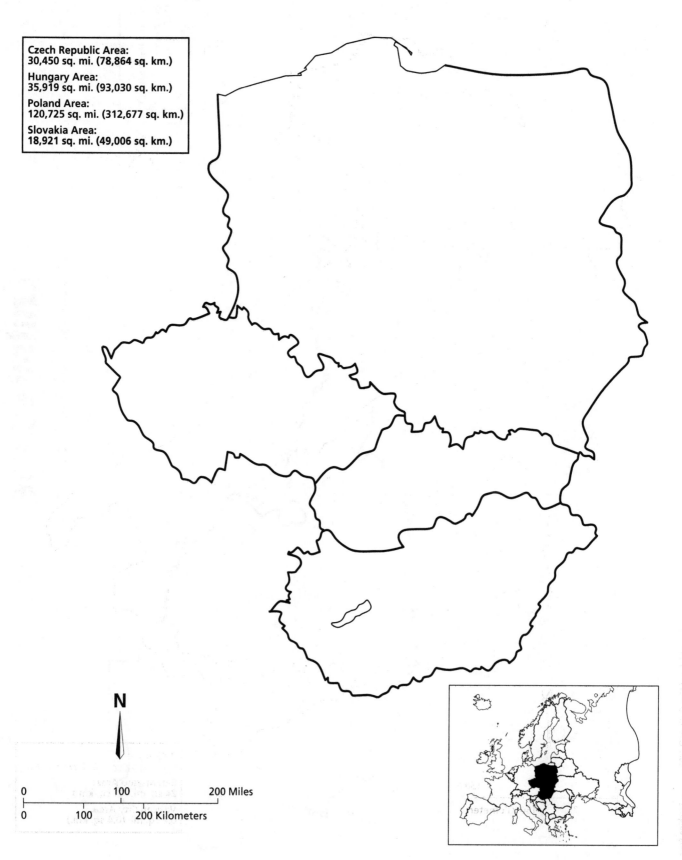

Czech Republic Area:
30,450 sq. mi. (78,864 sq. km.)

Hungary Area:
35,919 sq. mi. (93,030 sq. km.)

Poland Area:
120,725 sq. mi. (312,677 sq. km.)

Slovakia Area:
18,921 sq. mi. (49,006 sq. km.)

N

| 0 | | 100 | | 200 Miles |
| 0 | 100 | | 200 Kilometers | |

U.S. and World Map Outlines © 2004 Creative Teaching Press

Southern Europe

ITALY, SICILY, SARDINIA, SAN MARINO, VATICAN CITY

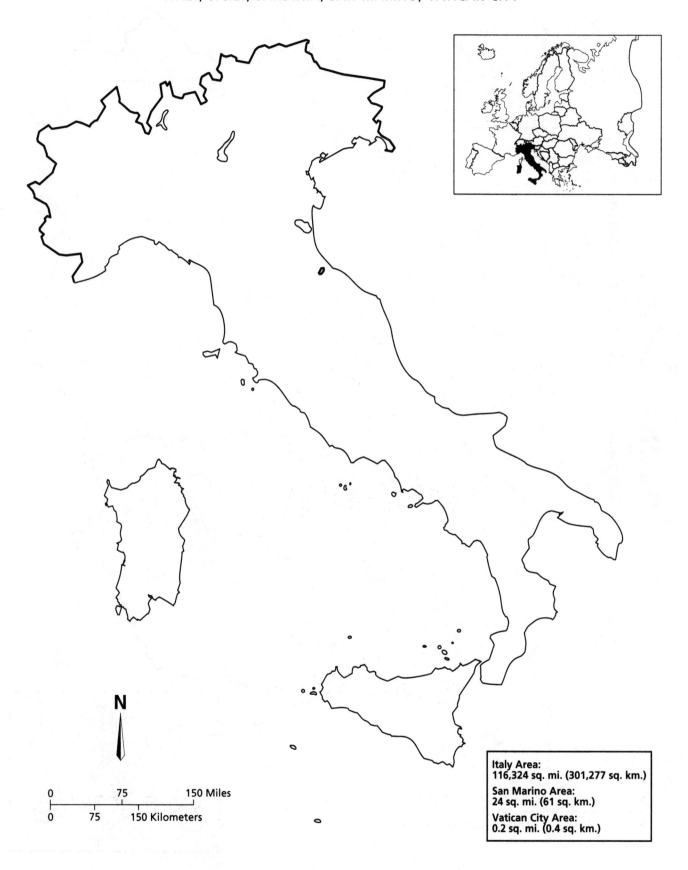

N

| 0 | 75 | 150 Miles |

| 0 | 75 | 150 Kilometers |

Italy Area:
116,324 sq. mi. (301,277 sq. km.)

San Marino Area:
24 sq. mi. (61 sq. km.)

Vatican City Area:
0.2 sq. mi. (0.4 sq. km.)

Southern Europe

SLOVENIA, CROATIA, BOSNIA-HERZEGOVINA, SERBIA-MONTENEGRO

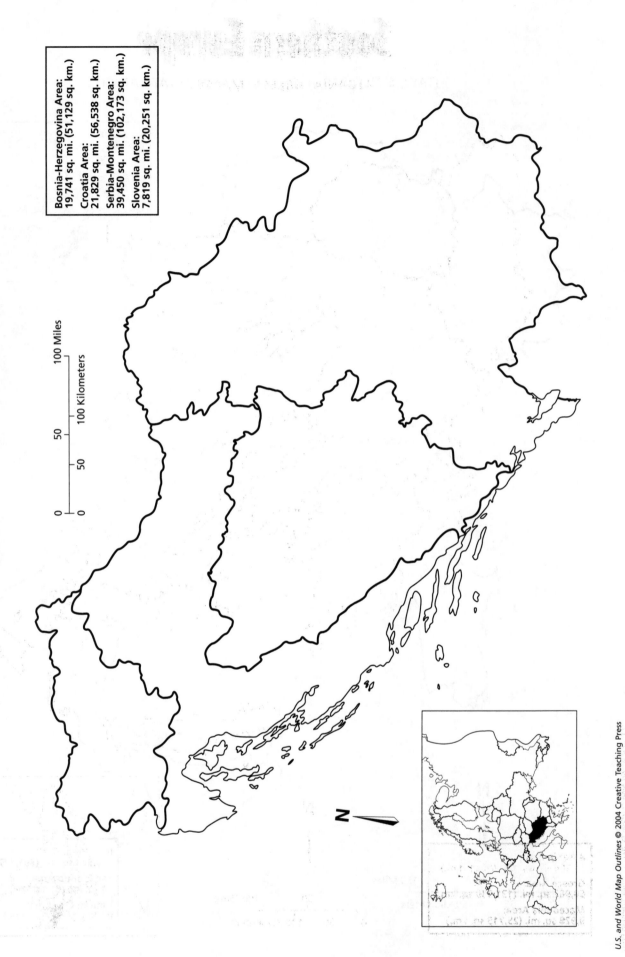

Bosnia-Herzegovina Area:
19,741 sq. mi. (51,129 sq. km.)

Croatia Area:
21,829 sq. mi. (56,538 sq. km.)

Serbia-Montenegro Area:
39,450 sq. mi. (102,173 sq. km.)

Slovenia Area:
7,819 sq. mi. (20,251 sq. km.)

100 Miles

100 Kilometers

N

Southern Europe

ALBANIA, GREECE, MACEDONIA

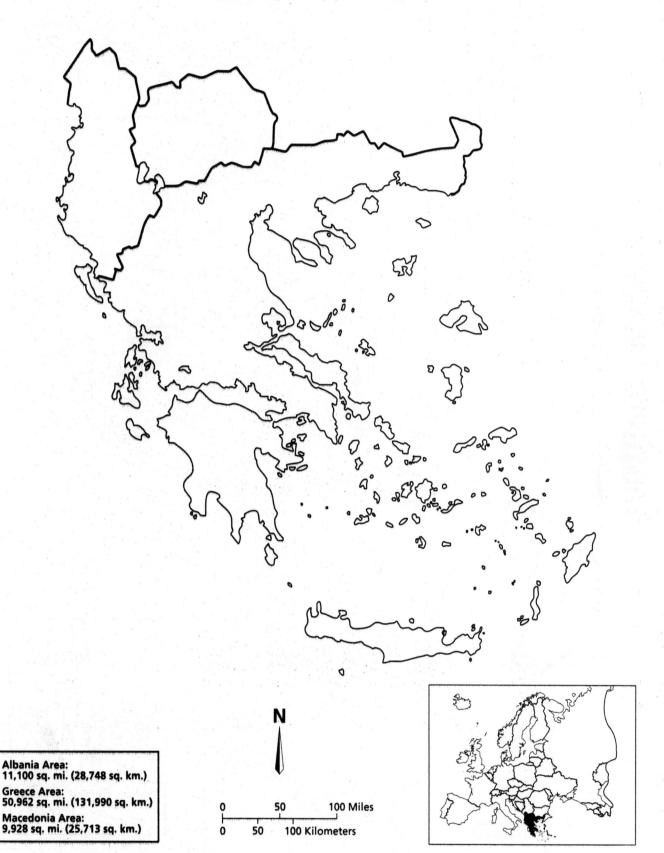

N

Albania Area:
11,100 sq. mi. (28,748 sq. km.)

Greece Area:
50,962 sq. mi. (131,990 sq. km.)

Macedonia Area:
9,928 sq. mi. (25,713 sq. km.)

| 0 | | 50 | | 100 Miles |
| 0 | 50 | | 100 Kilometers | |

Eastern Europe

ESTONIA, LATVIA, LITHUANIA

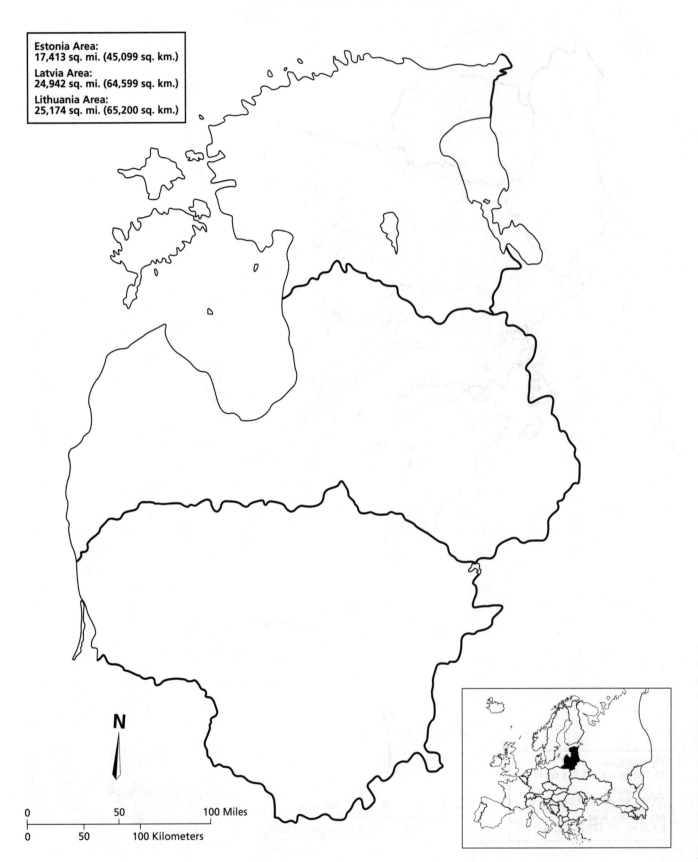

Estonia Area:
17,413 sq. mi. (45,099 sq. km.)
Latvia Area:
24,942 sq. mi. (64,599 sq. km.)
Lithuania Area:
25,174 sq. mi. (65,200 sq. km.)

N

| 0 | 50 | 100 Miles |
| 0 | 50 | 100 Kilometers |

Eastern Europe

BELARUS, UKRAINE

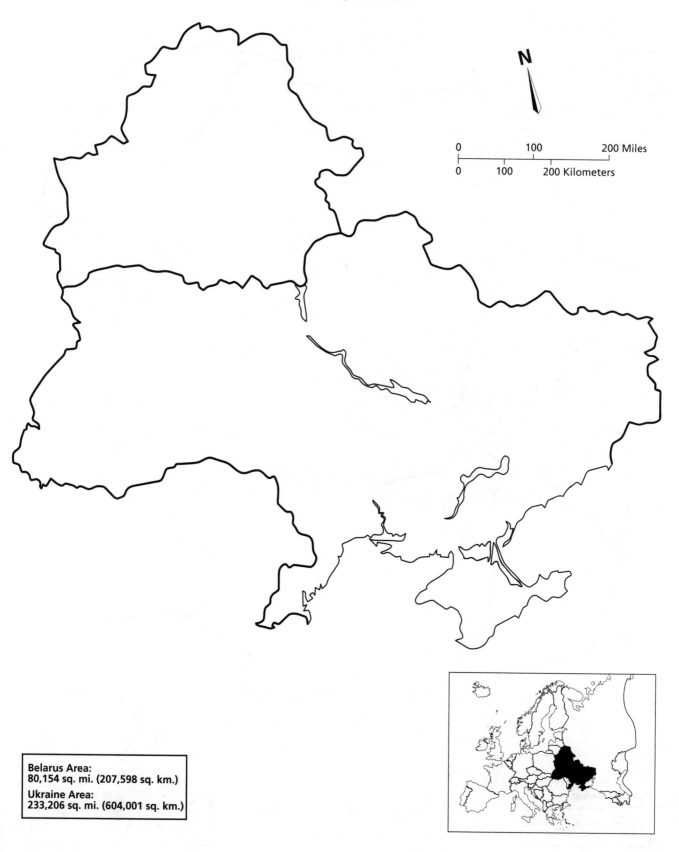

N

| 0 | | 100 | | 200 Miles |
| 0 | 100 | | 200 Kilometers | |

Belarus Area:
80,154 sq. mi. (207,598 sq. km.)

Ukraine Area:
233,206 sq. mi. (604,001 sq. km.)

Southeastern Europe

ROMANIA, BULGARIA, MOLDOVA

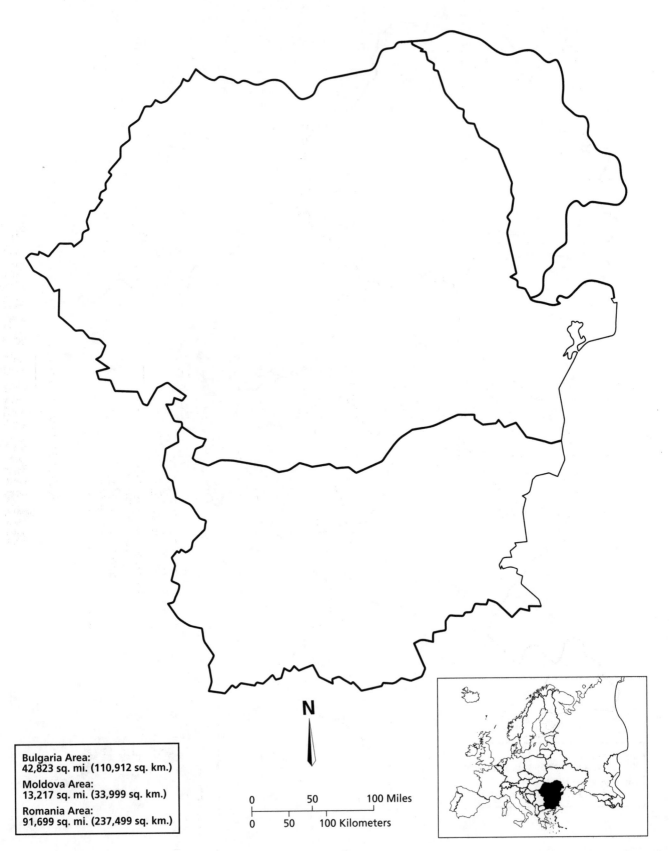

N

Bulgaria Area:
42,823 sq. mi. (110,912 sq. km.)

Moldova Area:
13,217 sq. mi. (33,999 sq. km.)

Romania Area:
91,699 sq. mi. (237,499 sq. km.)

0   50   100 Miles

0   50   100 Kilometers

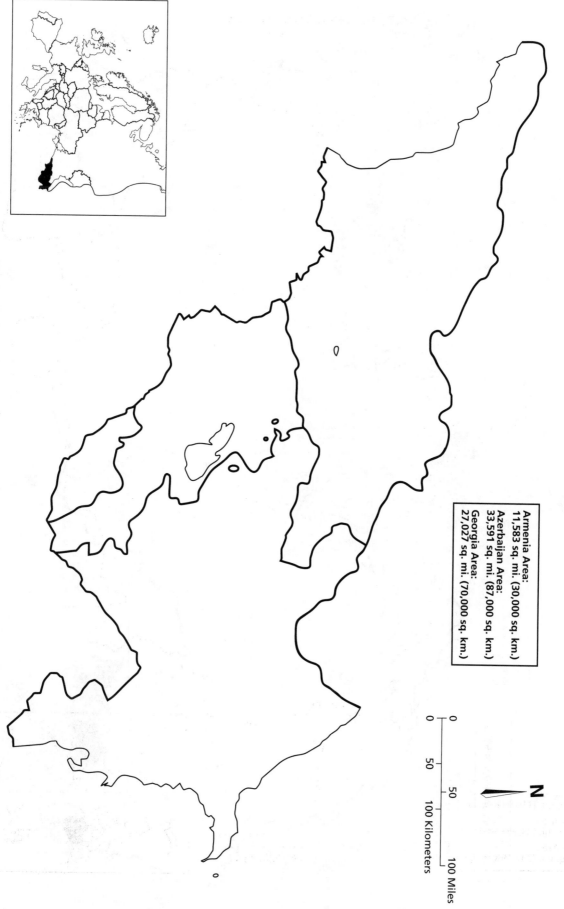

Southeastern Europe

GEORGIA, ARMENIA, AZERBAIJAN

Armenia Area:
11,583 sq. mi. (30,000 sq. km.)
Azerbaijan Area:
33,591 sq. mi. (87,000 sq. km.)
Georgia Area:
27,027 sq. mi. (70,000 sq. km.)

N

0   50   50   100 Kilometers

0   50   100 Miles

Northern Asia

RUSSIA

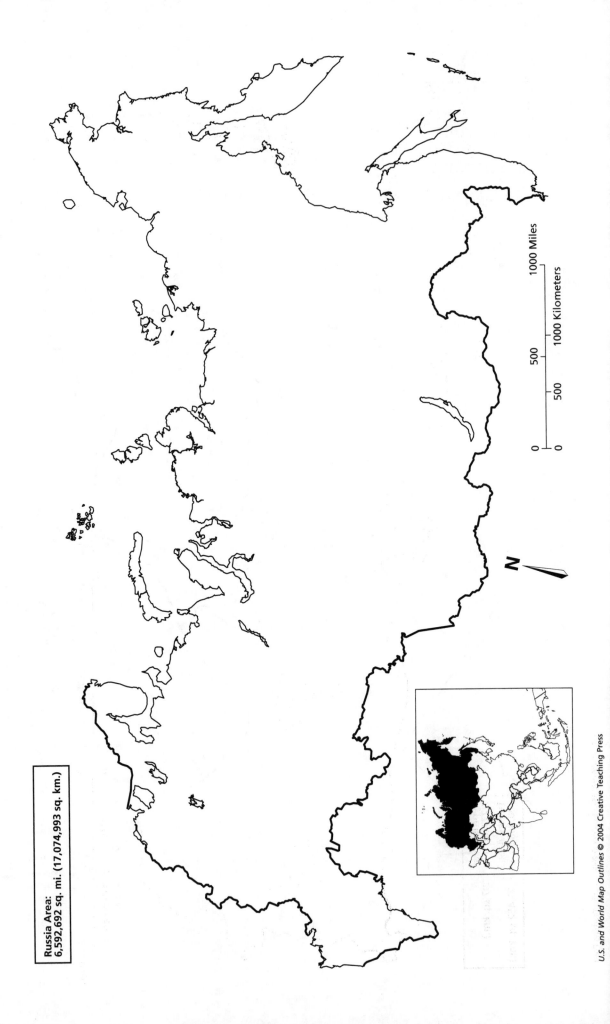

Russia Area:
6,592,692 sq. mi. (17,074,993 sq. km.)

N

1000 Miles

1000 Kilometers

500

500

0

0

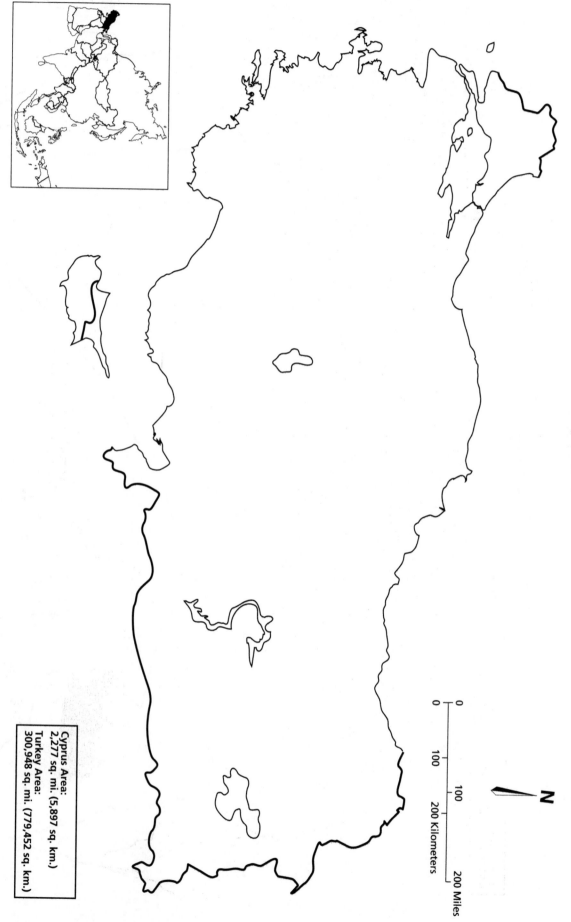

Middle East

TURKEY, CYPRUS

N

0
0
100
100
200 Kilometers
200 Miles

Cyprus Area:
2,277 sq. mi. (5,897 sq. km.)
Turkey Area:
300,948 sq. mi. (779,452 sq. km.)

Middle East

ISRAEL, JORDAN, LEBANON, SYRIA, IRAQ

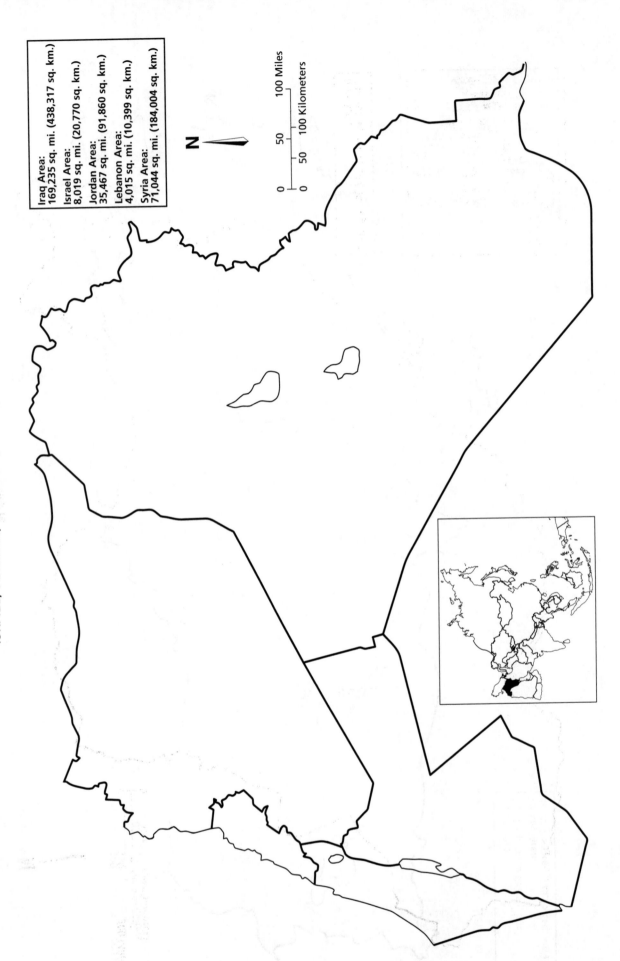

Iraq Area:
169,235 sq. mi. (438,317 sq. km.)

Israel Area:
8,019 sq. mi. (20,770 sq. km.)

Jordan Area:
35,467 sq. mi. (91,860 sq. km.)

Lebanon Area:
4,015 sq. mi. (10,399 sq. km.)

Syria Area:
71,044 sq. mi. (184,004 sq. km.)

N

100 Miles
100 Kilometers
50
50
50
0
0

54

Middle East

IRAN

N

0
0
100
100
100
200 Kilometers
200 Miles

Middle East

SAUDI ARABIA, QATAR, BAHRAIN, KUWAIT, UNITED ARAB EMIRATES, YEMEN, OMAN

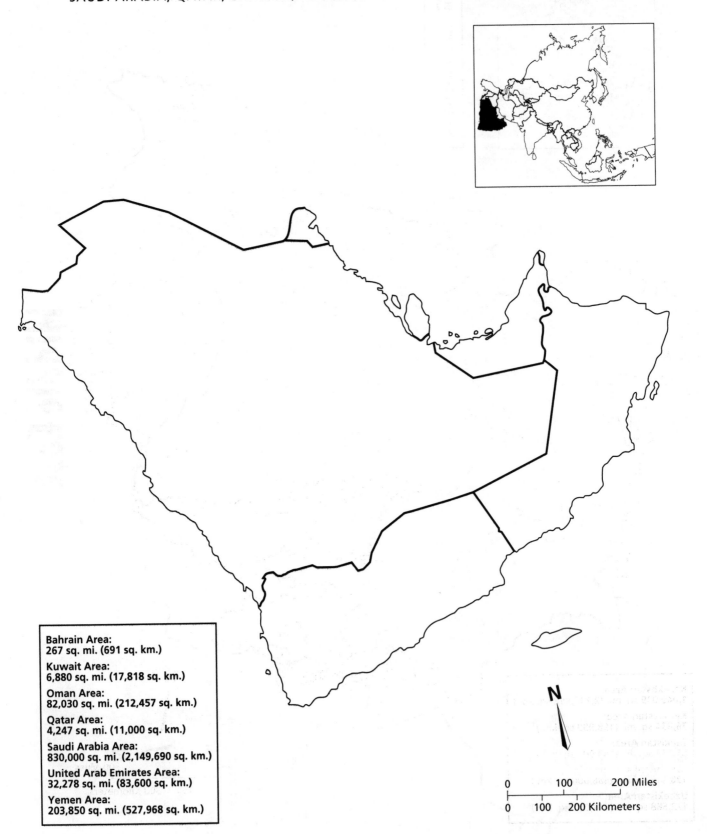

Bahrain Area:
267 sq. mi. (691 sq. km.)

Kuwait Area:
6,880 sq. mi. (17,818 sq. km.)

Oman Area:
82,030 sq. mi. (212,457 sq. km.)

Qatar Area:
4,247 sq. mi. (11,000 sq. km.)

Saudi Arabia Area:
830,000 sq. mi. (2,149,690 sq. km.)

United Arab Emirates Area:
32,278 sq. mi. (83,600 sq. km.)

Yemen Area:
203,850 sq. mi. (527,968 sq. km.)

N

| 0 | 100 | 200 Miles |
| 0 | 100 | 200 Kilometers |

Central Asia

KAZAKHSTAN, TURKMENISTAN, UZBEKISTAN, TAJIKISTAN, KYRGYZSTAN

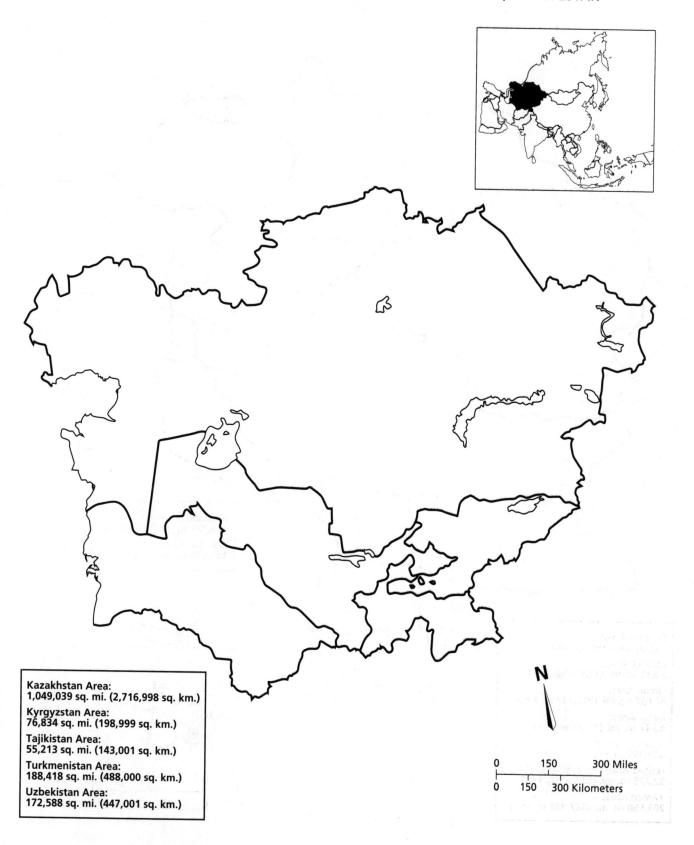

Kazakhstan Area:
1,049,039 sq. mi. (2,716,998 sq. km.)

Kyrgyzstan Area:
76,834 sq. mi. (198,999 sq. km.)

Tajikistan Area:
55,213 sq. mi. (143,001 sq. km.)

Turkmenistan Area:
188,418 sq. mi. (488,000 sq. km.)

Uzbekistan Area:
172,588 sq. mi. (447,001 sq. km.)

N

| 0 | | 150 | | 300 Miles |
| 0 | 150 | | 300 Kilometers | |

Southern Asia

AFGHANISTAN, PAKISTAN

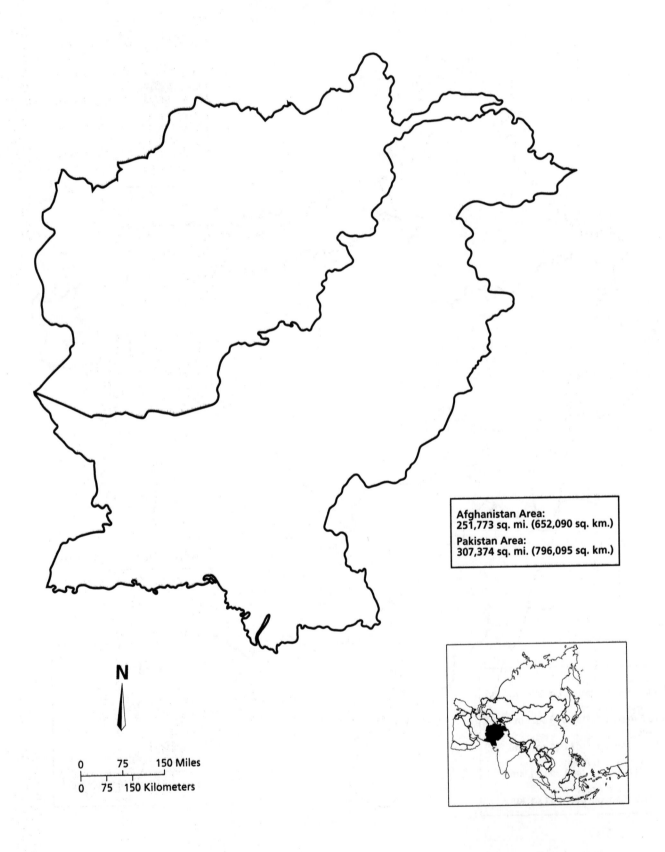

Afghanistan Area:
251,773 sq. mi. (652,090 sq. km.)

Pakistan Area:
307,374 sq. mi. (796,095 sq. km.)

N

| 0 | 75 | 150 Miles |

| 0 | 75 | 150 Kilometers |

Southern Asia

INDIA, BANGLADESH, NEPAL, BHUTAN, SRI LANKA

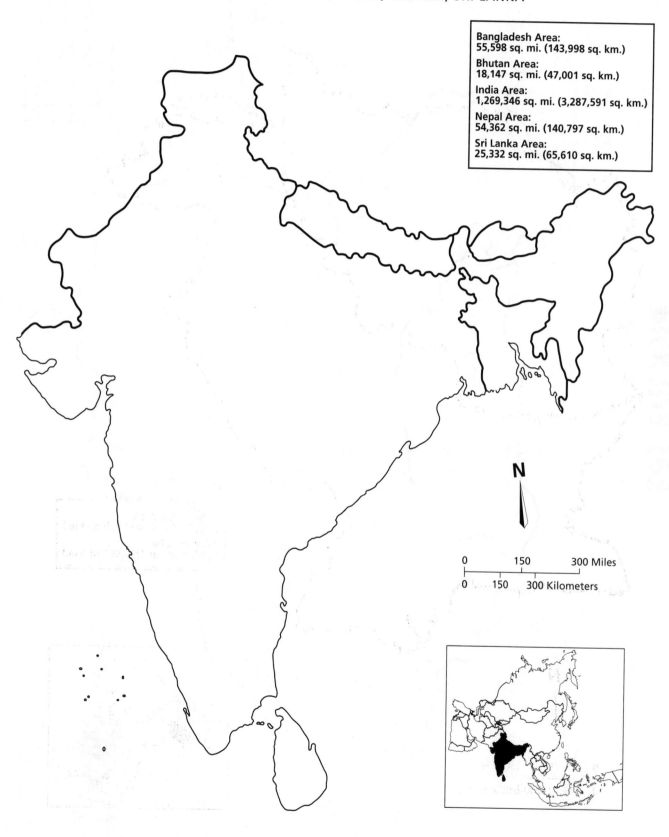

Bangladesh Area:
55,598 sq. mi. (143,998 sq. km.)

Bhutan Area:
18,147 sq. mi. (47,001 sq. km.)

India Area:
1,269,346 sq. mi. (3,287,591 sq. km.)

Nepal Area:
54,362 sq. mi. (140,797 sq. km.)

Sri Lanka Area:
25,332 sq. mi. (65,610 sq. km.)

N

| 0 | 150 | 300 Miles |

| 0 | 150 | 300 Kilometers |

Eastern Asia

CHINA, MONGOLIA, TAIWAN

N

	300 Miles
0 150	
0 150	300 Kilometers

China Area:
3,705,820 sq. mi. (9,598,032 sq. km.)

Mongolia Area:
604,250 sq. mi. (1,565,000 sq. km.)

Taiwan Area:
13,900 sq. mi. (36,000 sq. km.)

Eastern Asia

NORTH KOREA, SOUTH KOREA, JAPAN

Japan Area:
145,875 sq. mi. (377,815 sq. km.)
North Korea Area:
46,540 sq. mi. (120,538 sq. km.)
South Korea Area:
38,230 sq. mi. (99,016 sq. km.)

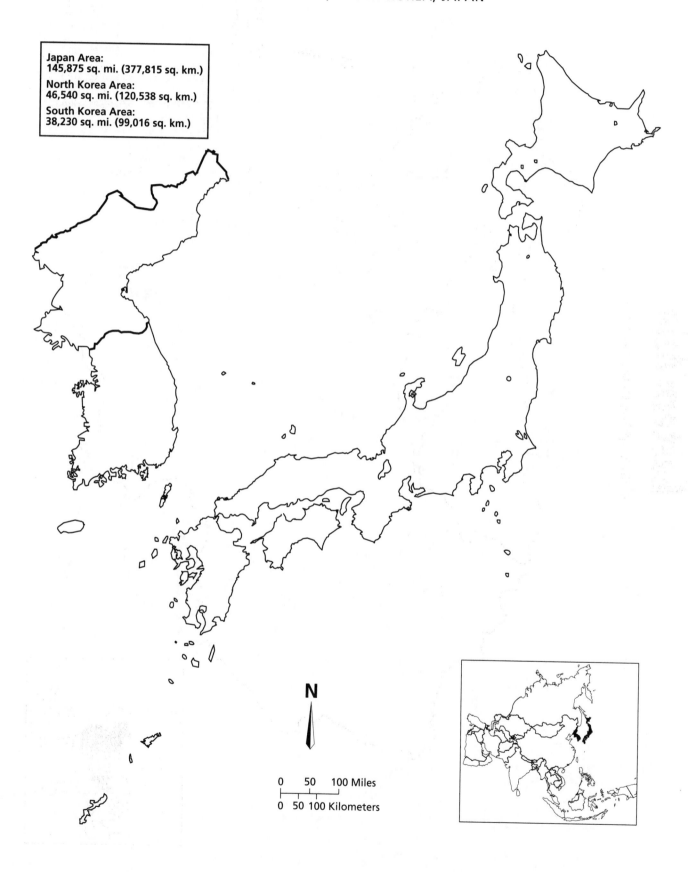

N

| 0 | 50 | 100 Miles |
| 0 | 50 | 100 Kilometers |

Southeastern Asia

MYANMAR, THAILAND, LAOS, CAMBODIA, VIETNAM

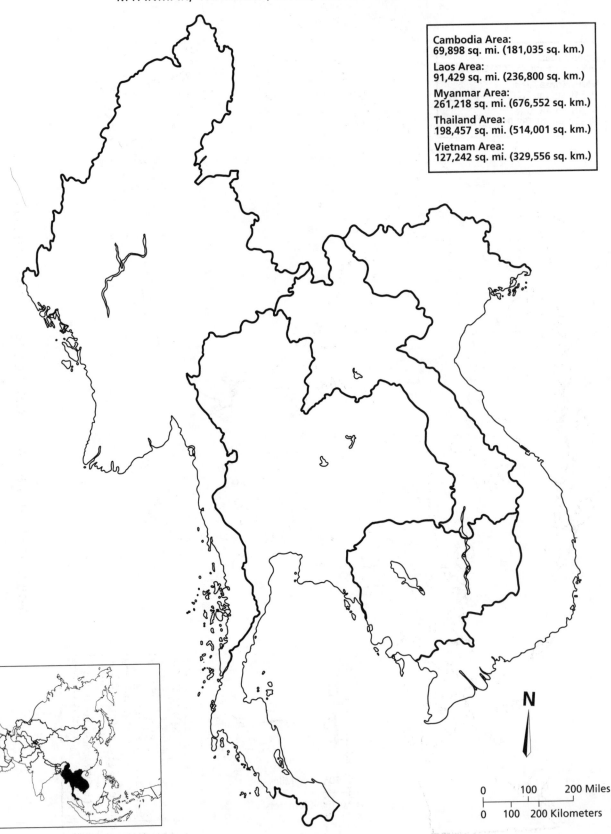

Cambodia Area:
69,898 sq. mi. (181,035 sq. km.)

Laos Area:
91,429 sq. mi. (236,800 sq. km.)

Myanmar Area:
261,218 sq. mi. (676,552 sq. km.)

Thailand Area:
198,457 sq. mi. (514,001 sq. km.)

Vietnam Area:
127,242 sq. mi. (329,556 sq. km.)

N

0   100   200 Miles

0   100   200 Kilometers

Southeastern Asia

PHILIPPINES, MALAYSIA, SINGAPORE, INDONESIA, EAST TIMOR

East Timor Area:
5,641 sq. mi. (14,609 sq. km.)

Indonesia Area:
741,101 sq. mi. (1,919,443 sq. km.)

Malaysia Area:
127,317 sq. mi. (329,749 sq. km.)

Philippines Area:
115,831 sq. mi. (300,001 sq. km.)

Singapore Area:
239 sq. mi. (618 sq. km.)

N

0   200   400 Miles

0   200   400 Kilometers

Northern South America

COLOMBIA, VENEZUELA, TRINIDAD AND TOBAGO

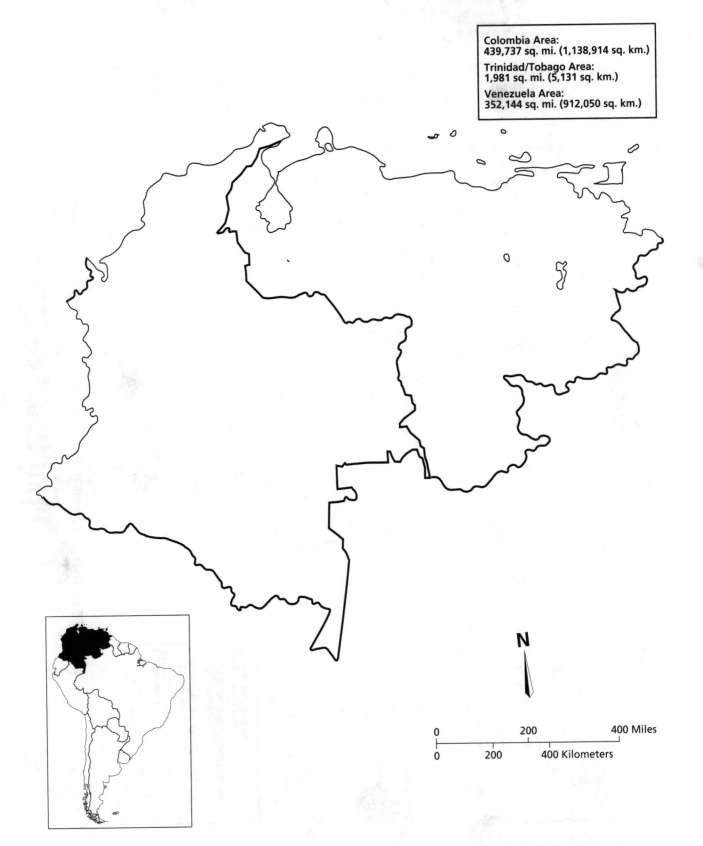

Colombia Area:
439,737 sq. mi. (1,138,914 sq. km.)

Trinidad/Tobago Area:
1,981 sq. mi. (5,131 sq. km.)

Venezuela Area:
352,144 sq. mi. (912,050 sq. km.)

N

0		200		400 Miles
0	200		400 Kilometers	

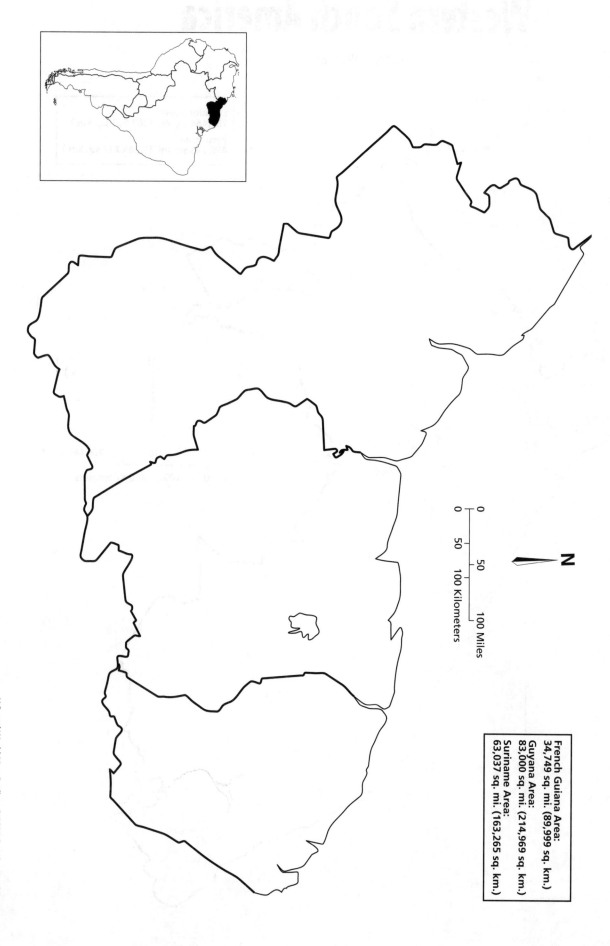

Northern South America

GUYANA, SURINAME, FRENCH GUIANA

N

0   50   100 Miles

0   50   100 Kilometers

French Guiana Area:
34,749 sq. mi. (89,999 sq. km.)
Guyana Area:
83,000 sq. mi. (214,969 sq. km.)
Suriname Area:
63,037 sq. mi. (163,265 sq. km.)

Western South America

ECUADOR, PERU

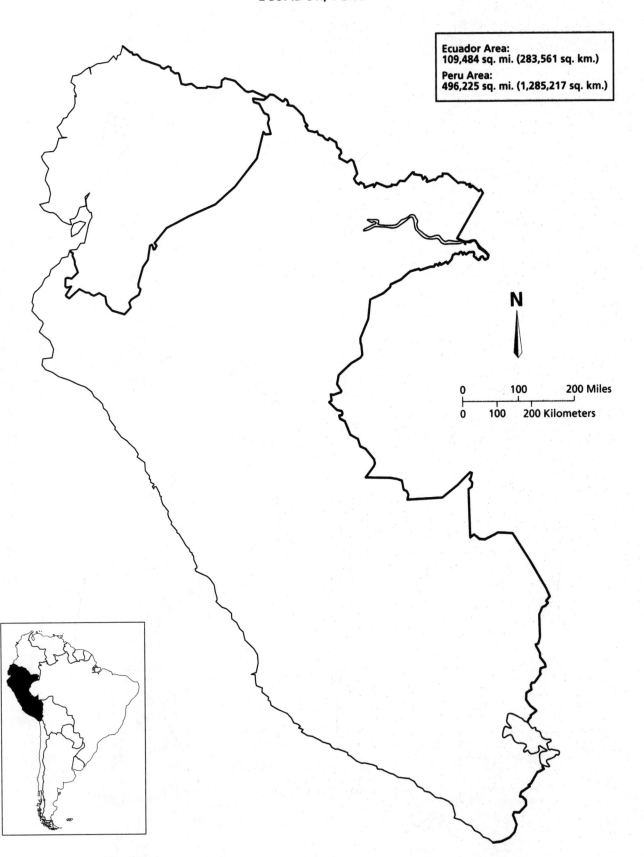

Ecuador Area:
109,484 sq. mi. (283,561 sq. km.)

Peru Area:
496,225 sq. mi. (1,285,217 sq. km.)

N

0		100		200 Miles
0	100	200 Kilometers		

U.S. and World Map Outlines © 2004 Creative Teaching Press

Central South America

BOLIVIA, PARAGUAY

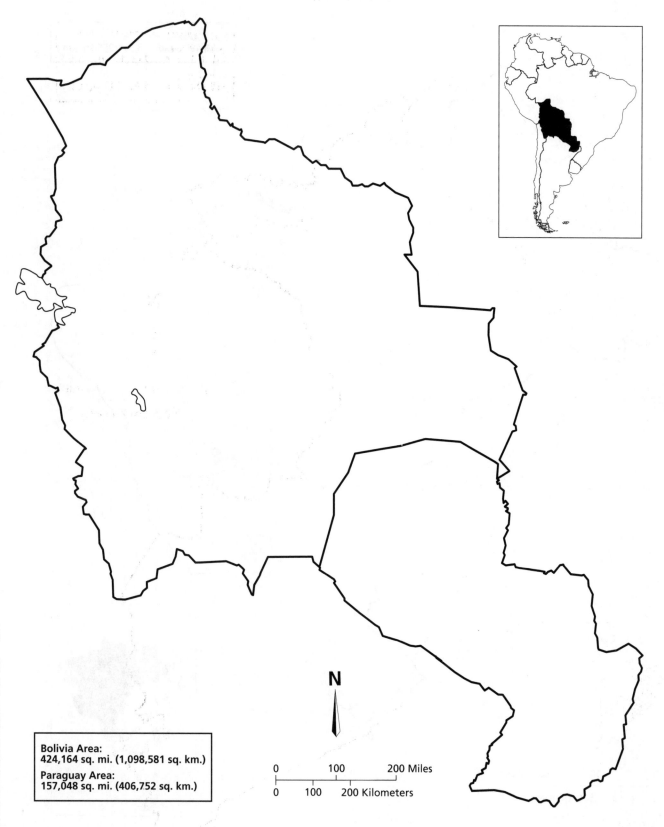

N

Bolivia Area:
424,164 sq. mi. (1,098,581 sq. km.)

Paraguay Area:
157,048 sq. mi. (406,752 sq. km.)

0   100   200 Miles

0   100   200 Kilometers

Eastern South America

BRAZIL

Brazil Area:
3,286,488 sq. mi. (8,511,965 sq. km.)

N

0   250   500 Miles
0   250   500 Kilometers

U.S. and World Map Outlines © 2004 Creative Teaching Press

Southern South America

CHILE, ARGENTINA, URUGUAY, FALKLAND ISLANDS

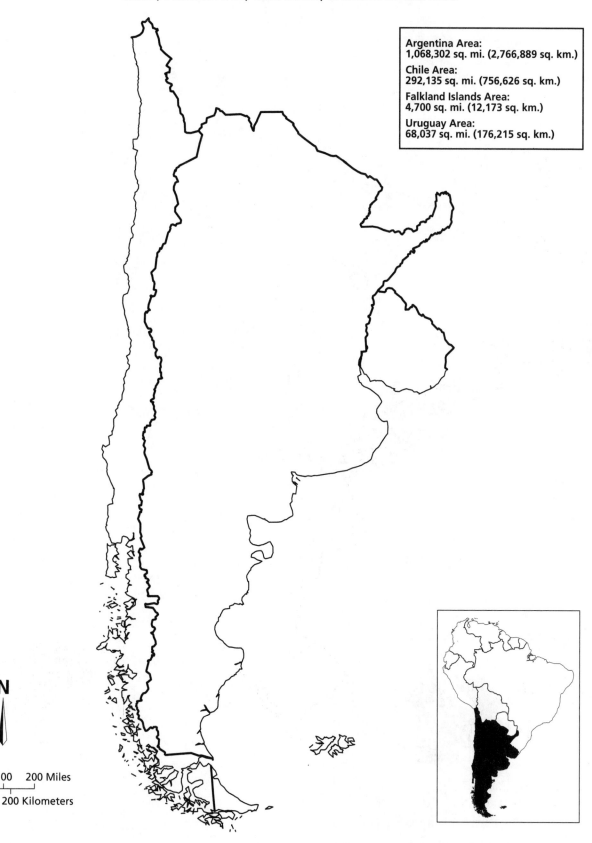

Argentina Area:
1,068,302 sq. mi. (2,766,889 sq. km.)

Chile Area:
292,135 sq. mi. (756,626 sq. km.)

Falkland Islands Area:
4,700 sq. mi. (12,173 sq. km.)

Uruguay Area:
68,037 sq. mi. (176,215 sq. km.)

N

| 0 | 100 | 200 Miles |
| 0 | 200 Kilometers | |

North America

CANADA AND GREENLAND

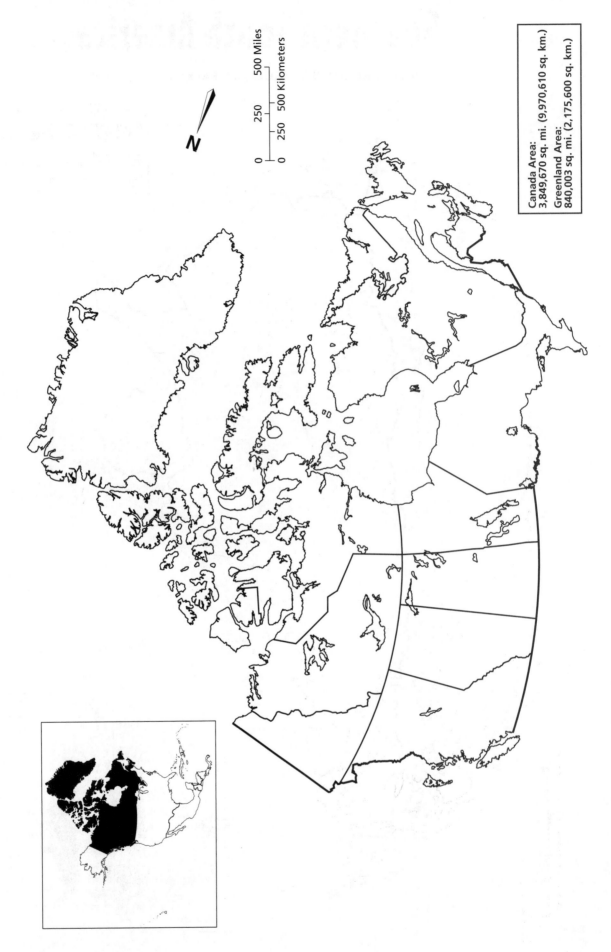

500 Miles

500 Kilometers

250

250

0

0

N

Canada Area:
3,849,670 sq. mi. (9,970,610 sq. km.)
Greenland Area:
840,003 sq. mi. (2,175,600 sq. km.)

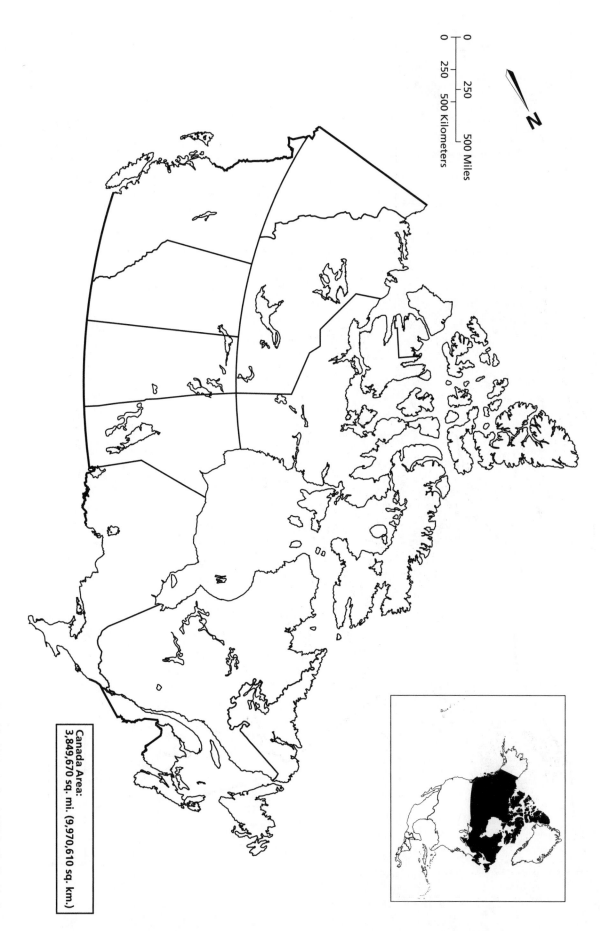

North America

CANADIAN PROVINCES AND TERRITORIES

0
0

250

250

500 Kilometers

500 Miles

N

Canada Area:
3,849,670 sq. mi. (9,970,610 sq. km.)

North America

MEXICO

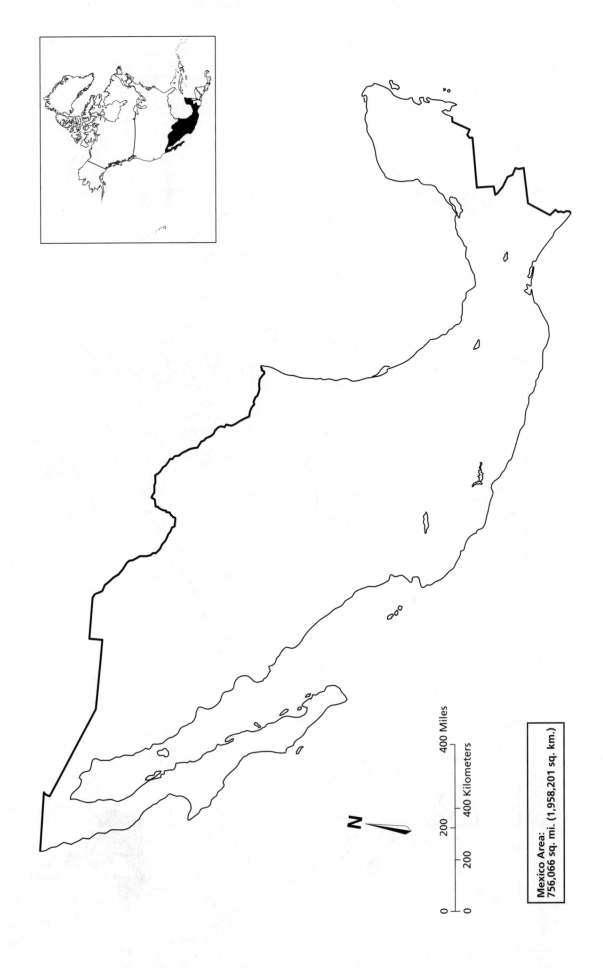

400 Miles

400 Kilometers

N

200

400

200

0

0

Mexico Area:
756,066 sq. mi. (1,958,201 sq. km.)

Caribbean

BAHAMAS, CUBA, JAMAICA, HAITI, DOMINICAN REPUBLIC

Bahamas Area:
5,382 sq. mi. (13,939 sq. km.)
Cuba Area:
42,804 sq. mi. (110,861 sq. km.)
Dominican Republic Area:
18,816 sq. mi. (48,734 sq. km.)
Haiti Area:
10,714 sq. mi. (27,750 sq. km.)
Jamaica Area:
4,244 sq. mi. (10,991 sq. km.)

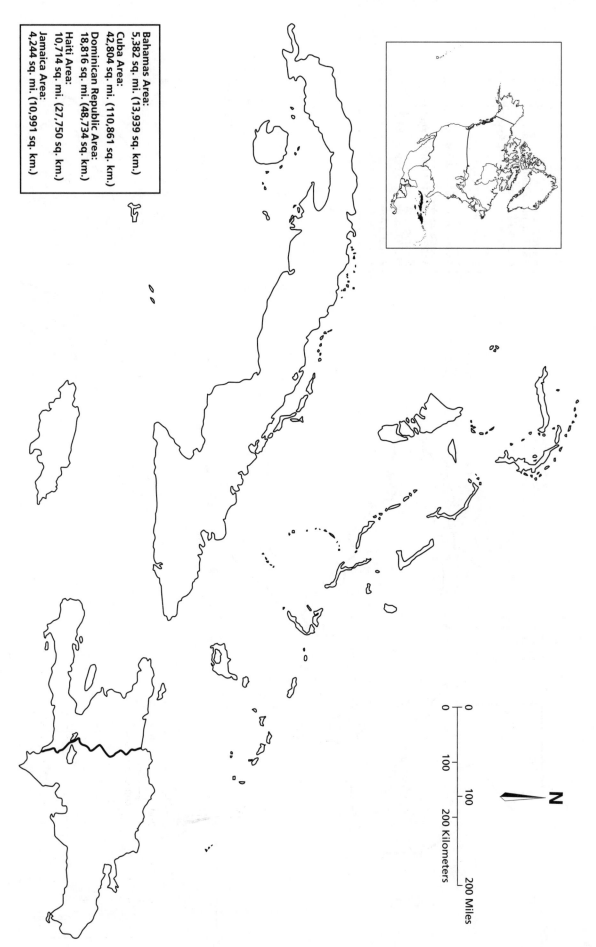

N

0
0

100

100

200 Kilometers

200 Miles

Central America

BELIZE, GUATEMALA, EL SALVADOR, HONDURAS, NICARAGUA, COSTA RICA, PANAMA

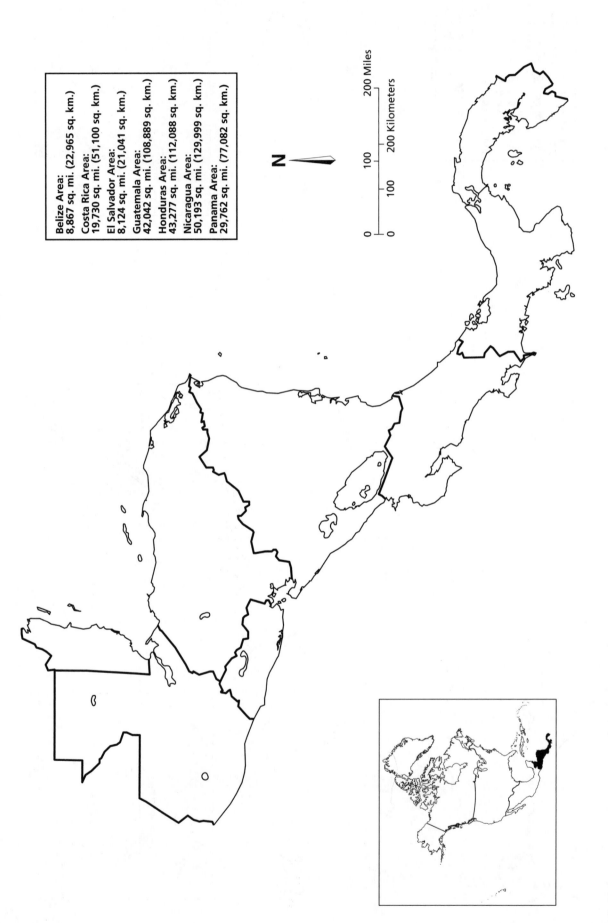

Belize Area:
8,867 sq. mi. (22,965 sq. km.)

Costa Rica Area:
19,730 sq. mi. (51,100 sq. km.)

El Salvador Area:
8,124 sq. mi. (21,041 sq. km.)

Guatemala Area:
42,042 sq. mi. (108,889 sq. km.)

Honduras Area:
43,277 sq. mi. (112,088 sq. km.)

Nicaragua Area:
50,193 sq. mi. (129,999 sq. km.)

Panama Area:
29,762 sq. mi. (77,082 sq. km.)

N

| 0 | 100 | 200 Miles |
| 0 | 100 | 200 | 200 Kilometers |

U.S. and World Map Outlines © 2004 Creative Teaching Press

Central America

PUERTO RICO

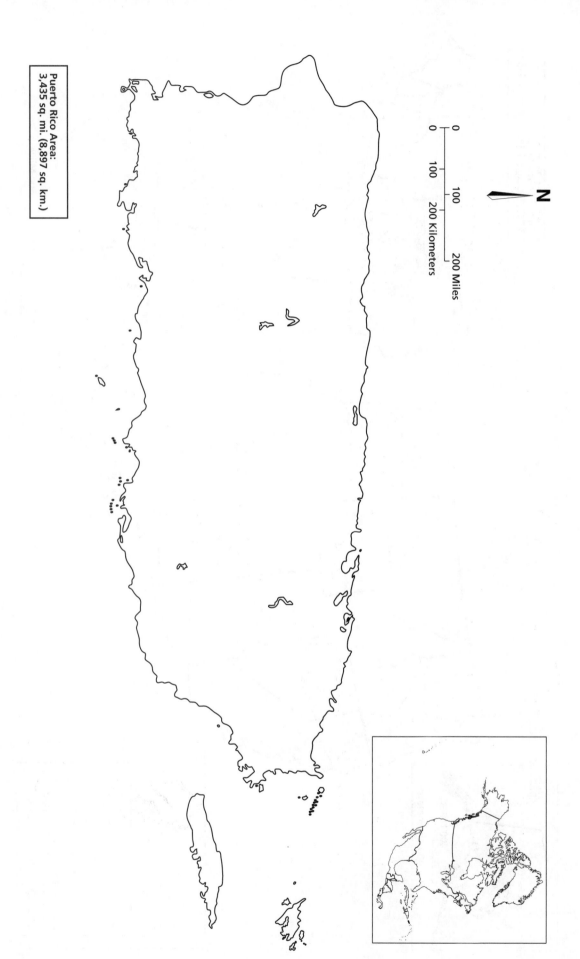

N

0
0
100
100
200 Kilometers
200 Miles

United States

United States Area:
3,717,796 sq. mi. (9,629,091 sq. km.)

N

250   500 Miles

250   500 Kilometers

0   0

400 Miles

400 Kilometers

0   0

100 Miles

100 Kilometers

0   0

76

U.S. and World Map Outlines © 2004 Creative Teaching Press

United States

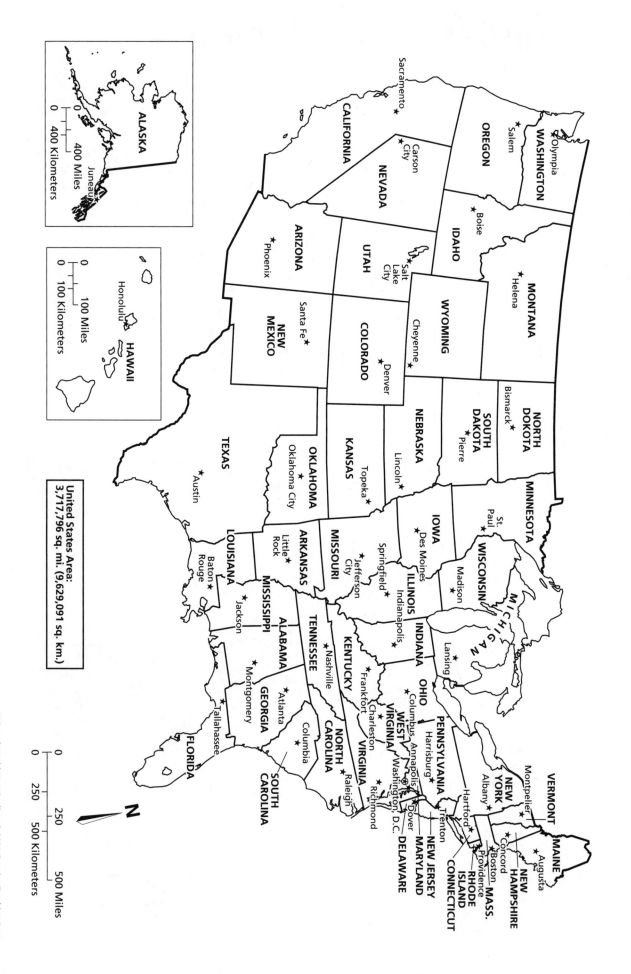

United States Area:
3,717,796 sq. mi. (9,629,091 sq. km.)

ALASKA
0 400 Miles
0 400 Kilometers
Juneau

HAWAII
Honolulu
0 100 Miles
0 100 Kilometers

WASHINGTON Olympia Salem **OREGON**

CALIFORNIA Sacramento Carson City **NEVADA**

IDAHO Boise

MONTANA Helena

ARIZONA Phoenix **UTAH** Salt Lake City

WYOMING Cheyenne

NORTH DAKOTA Bismarck

NEW MEXICO Santa Fe **COLORADO** Denver

SOUTH DAKOTA Pierre

NEBRASKA Lincoln

MINNESOTA

TEXAS Austin **OKLAHOMA** Oklahoma City **KANSAS** Topeka

IOWA Des Moines St. Paul

WISCONSIN Madison

MICHIGAN Lansing

LOUISIANA Baton Rouge **ARKANSAS** Little Rock **MISSOURI** Jefferson City Springfield

ILLINOIS Indianapolis **INDIANA**

MISSISSIPPI Jackson **ALABAMA** Montgomery **TENNESSEE** Nashville **KENTUCKY** Frankfort

OHIO Columbus **PENNSYLVANIA** Harrisburg

GEORGIA Atlanta **NORTH CAROLINA** Columbia Charleston **WEST VIRGINIA** **VIRGINIA** Richmond Annapolis Washington, D.C.

FLORIDA Tallahassee **SOUTH CAROLINA** Raleigh Dover **DELAWARE** **MARYLAND** **NEW JERSEY** Trenton

NEW YORK Albany Hartford **CONNECTICUT** Providence **RHODE ISLAND** Boston **MASS.** Concord **NEW HAMPSHIRE**

VERMONT Montpelier **MAINE** Augusta

N

0 250 500 Miles
0 250 500 Kilometers

U.S. and World Map Outlines © 2004 Creative Teaching Press

Thirteen Original Colonies

MAINE
(part of Mass.)

NEW
HAMPSHIRE

NEW
YORK

MASSACHUSETTS

RHODE
ISLAND

CONNECTICUT

PENNSYLVANIA

NEW JERSEY

DELAWARE

MARYLAND

VIRGINIA

NORTH
CAROLINA

SOUTH
CAROLINA

GEORGIA

N

| 0 | 100 | 200 Miles |
| 0 | 100 | 200 Kilometers |

Alabama

Alabama Area:
52,237 sq. mi. (135,293 sq. km.)

N

0		25		50 Miles
0	25		50 Kilometers	

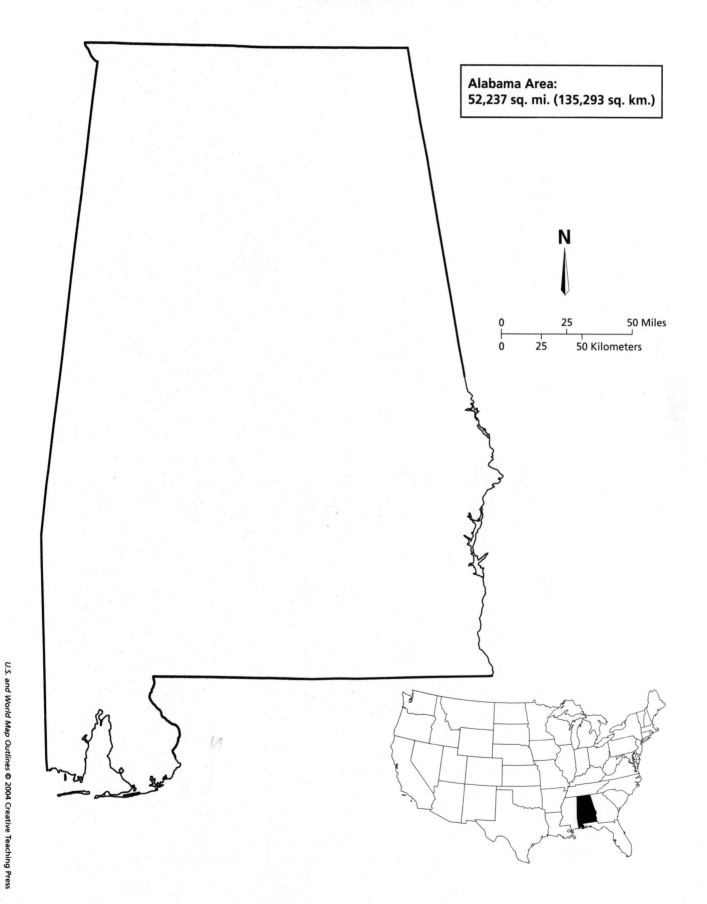

Alaska

Alaska Area:
615,230 sq. mi. (1,593,444 sq. km.)

N

0	100	200 Miles
0	100	200 Kilometers

Arizona

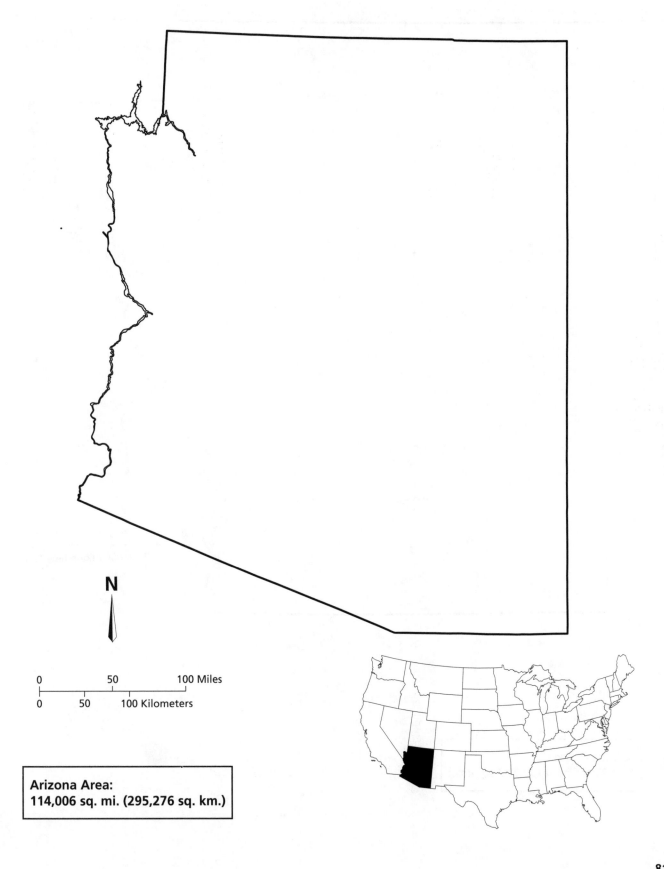

N

| 0 | 50 | 100 Miles |

| 0 | 50 | 100 Kilometers |

Arizona Area:
114,006 sq. mi. (295,276 sq. km.)

Arkansas

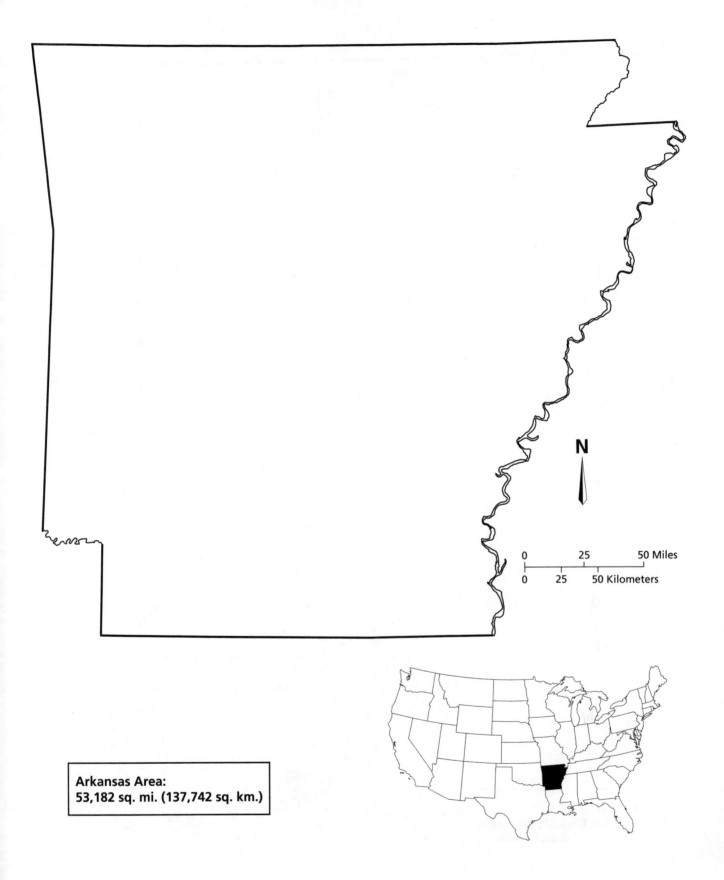

N

| 0 | 25 | 50 Miles |

| 0 | 25 | 50 Kilometers |

Arkansas Area:
53,182 sq. mi. (137,742 sq. km.)

California

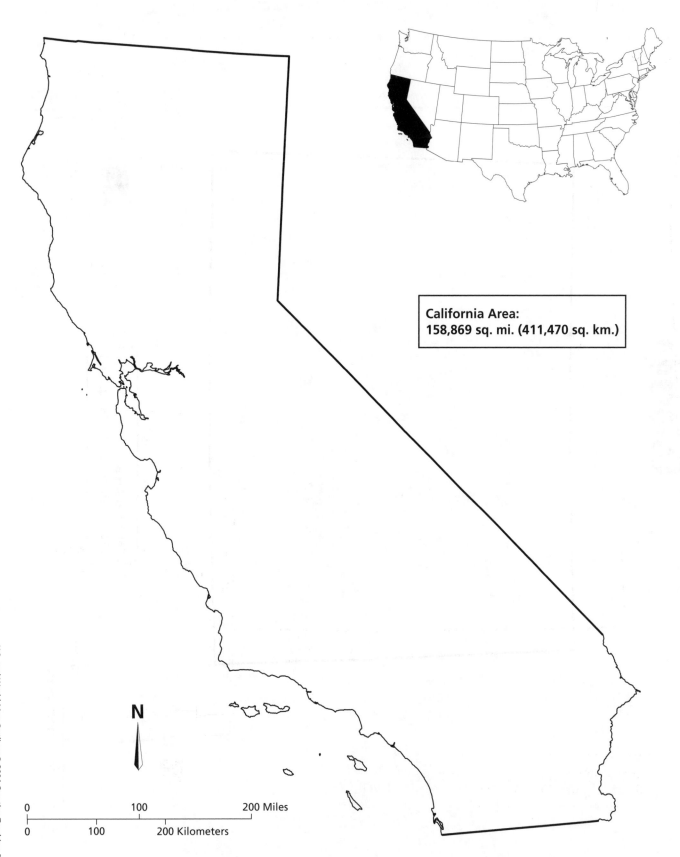

California Area:
158,869 sq. mi. (411,470 sq. km.)

N

0   100   200 Miles

0   100   200 Kilometers

Colorado

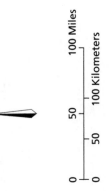

Colorado Area:
104,100 sq. mi. (269,618 sq. km.)

N

0	50	50	100 Miles
0	50	50	100 Kilometers

Connecticut

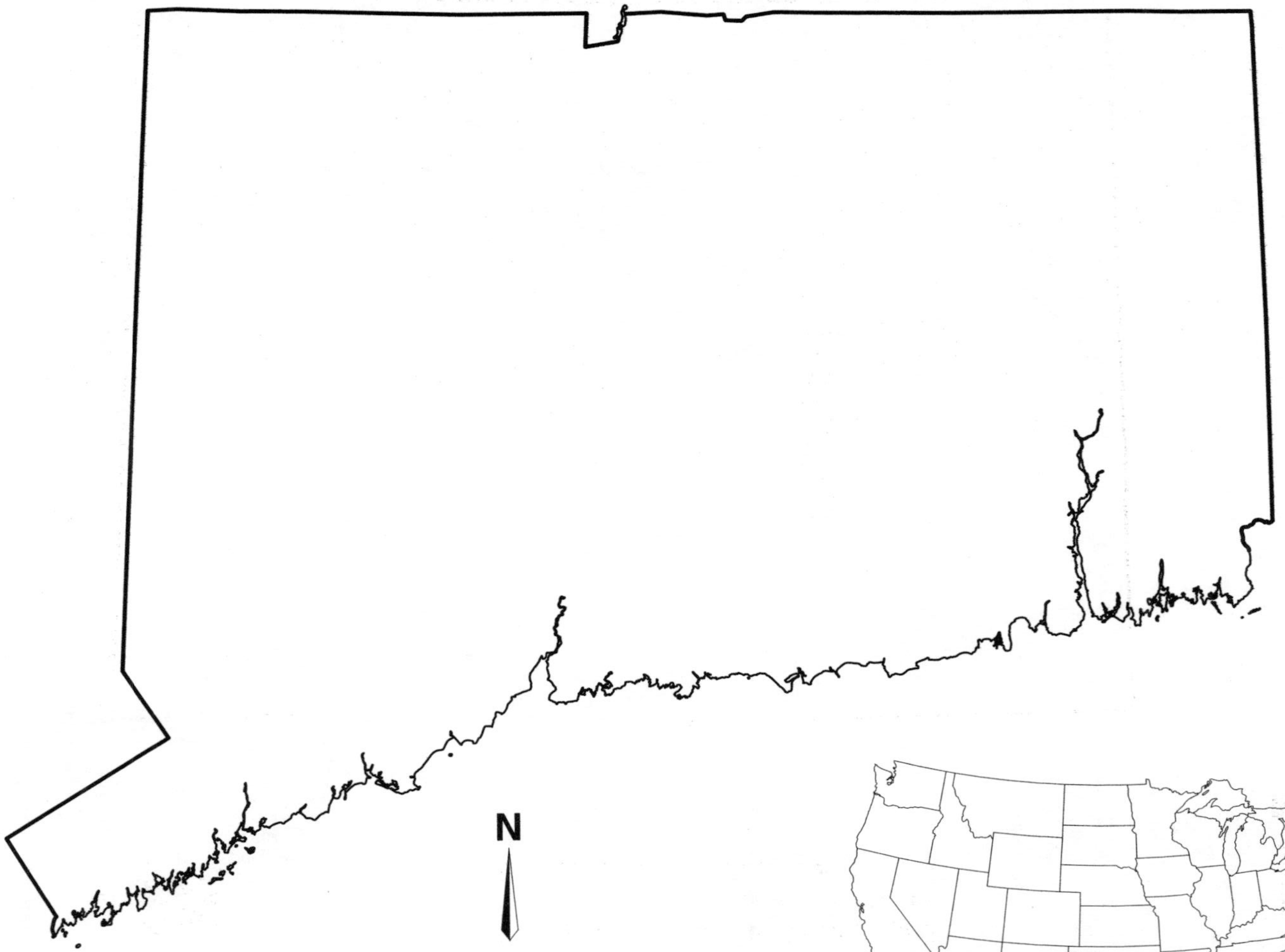

Connecticut Area:
5,544 sq. mi. (14,358 sq. km.)

N

0
0

10

10

20 Kilometers

20 Miles

U.S. and World Map Outlines © 2004 Creative Teaching Press

Delaware

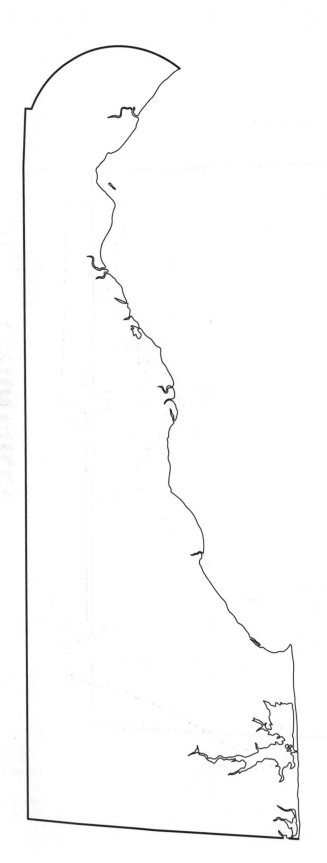

N

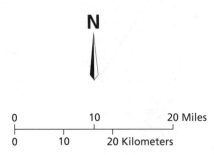

0		10		20 Miles
0	10		20 Kilometers	

Delaware Area:
2,396 sq. mi. (6,206 sq. km.)

Florida

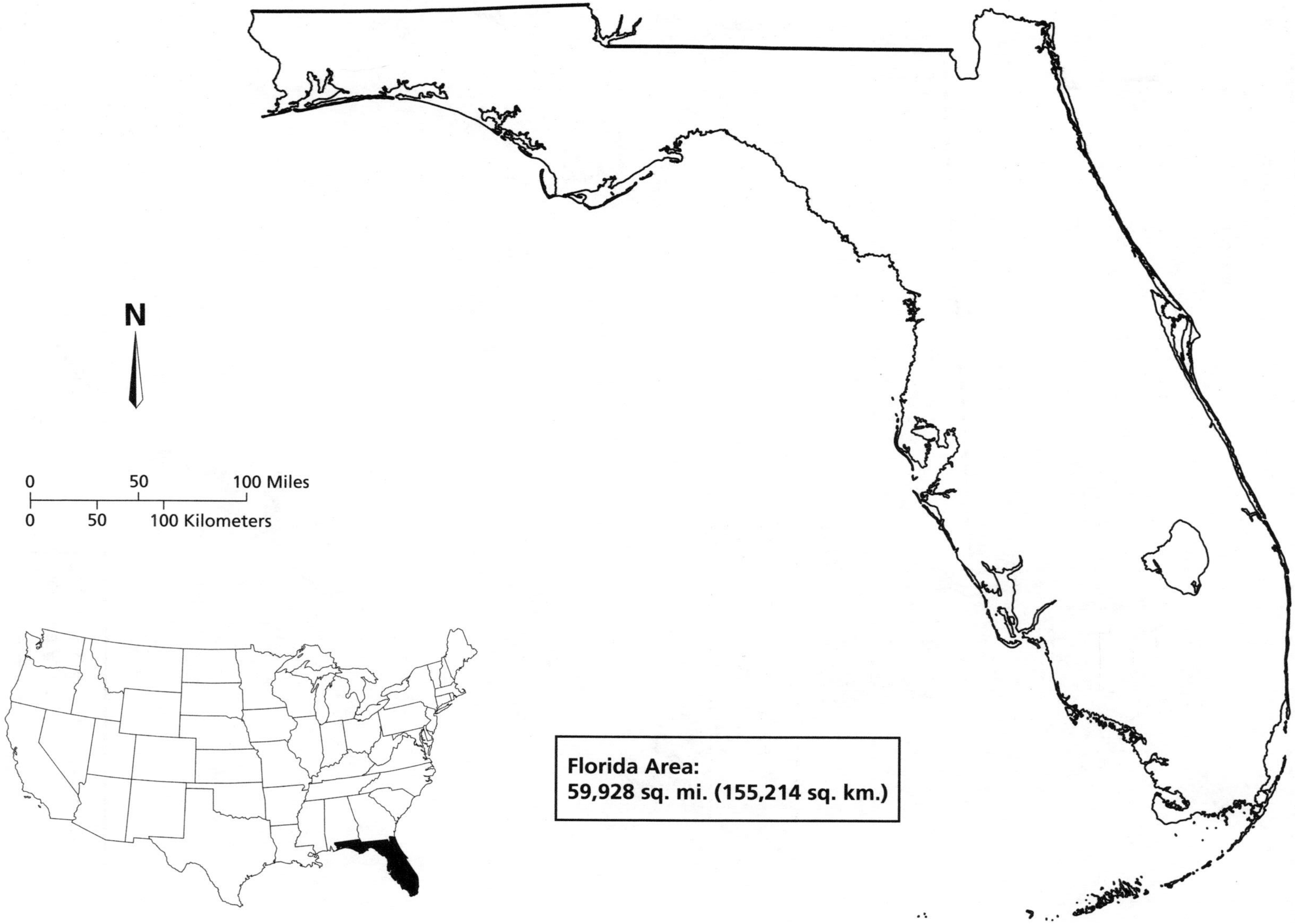

Florida Area:
59,928 sq. mi. (155,214 sq. km.)

N

0
0

50

50

100 Kilometers

100 Miles

Georgia

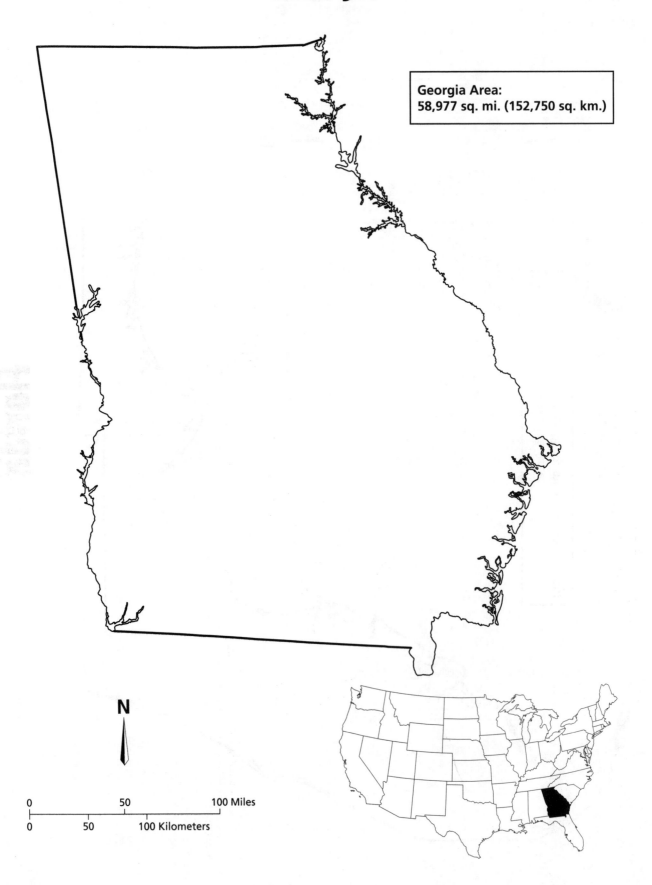

Georgia Area:
58,977 sq. mi. (152,750 sq. km.)

N

| 0 | | 50 | | 100 Miles |
| 0 | 50 | | 100 Kilometers | |

Hawaii

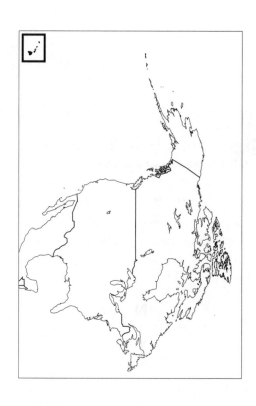

U.S. and World Map Outlines © 2004 Creative Teaching Press

Hawaii Area:
6,459 sq. mi. (16,729 sq. km.)

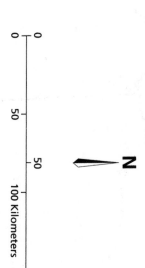

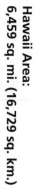

N

0   50   50   100 Miles

0   50   100 Kilometers

Idaho

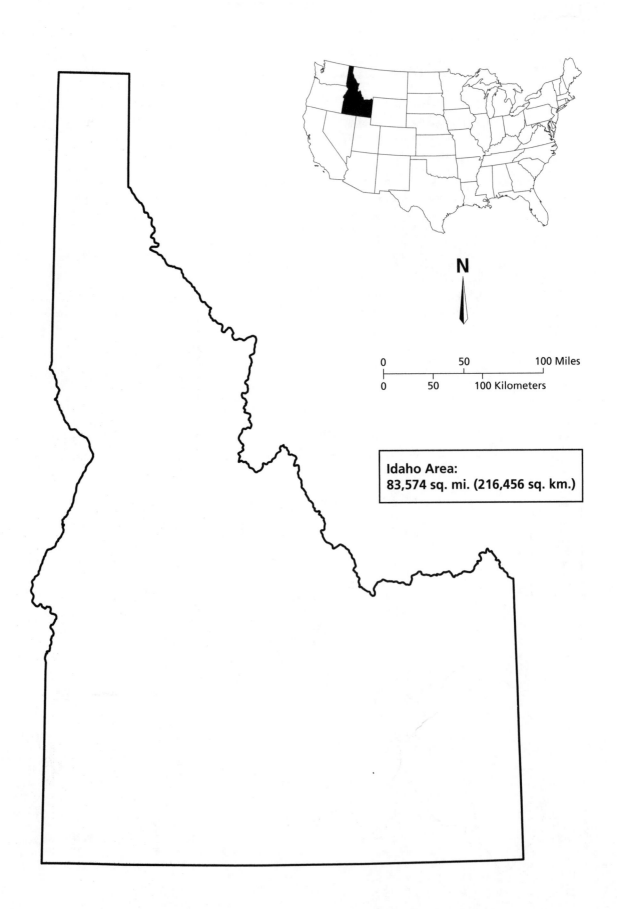

N

| 0 | | 50 | | 100 Miles |

| 0 | 50 | | 100 Kilometers |

Idaho Area:
83,574 sq. mi. (216,456 sq. km.)

Illinois

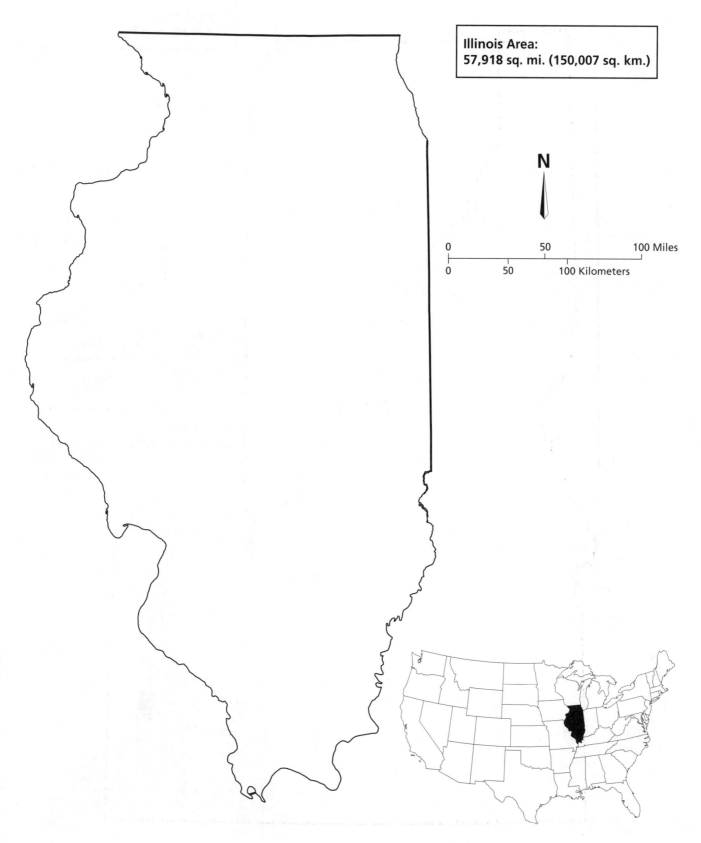

Illinois Area:
57,918 sq. mi. (150,007 sq. km.)

N

0   50   100 Miles
0   50   100 Kilometers

Indiana

Indiana Area:
36,420 sq. mi. (94,328 sq. km.)

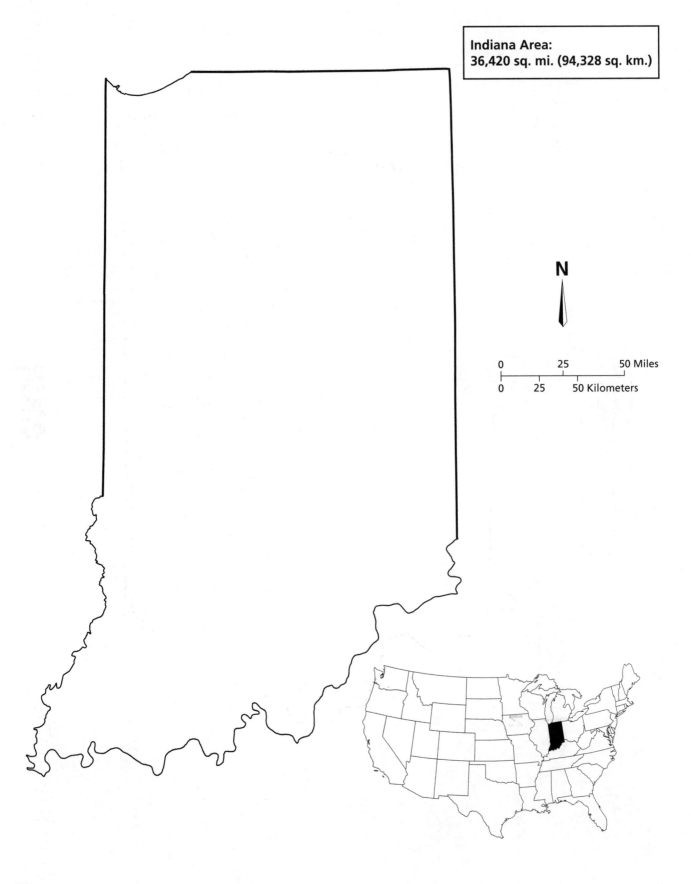

N

0		25		50 Miles
0	25		50 Kilometers	

Iowa

N

0 ———— 0
25 ———— 25
50 Kilometers ———— 50 Miles

Kansas

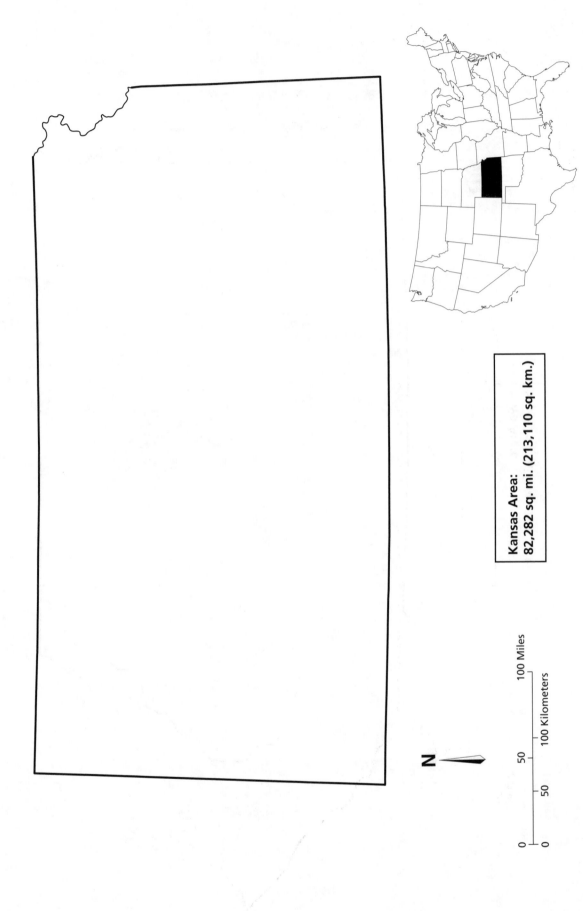

**Kansas Area:
82,282 sq. mi. (213,110 sq. km.)**

N

0	50	50	100 Miles	
0	50	100 Kilometers		

U.S. and World Map Outlines © 2004 Creative Teaching Press

Kentucky

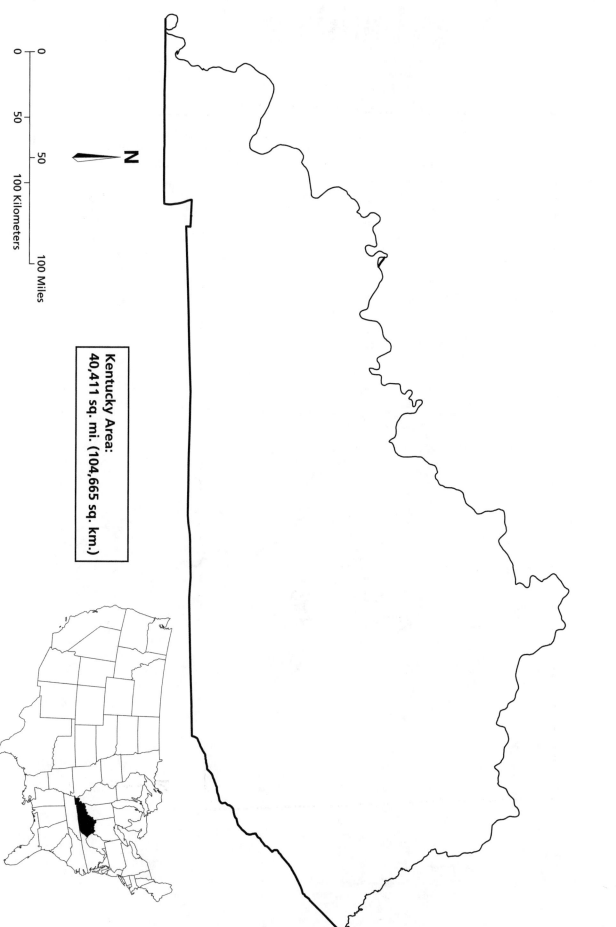

0
50
50
100 Kilometers

0
50
100 Miles

N

Kentucky Area:
40,411 sq. mi. (104,665 sq. km.)

Louisiana

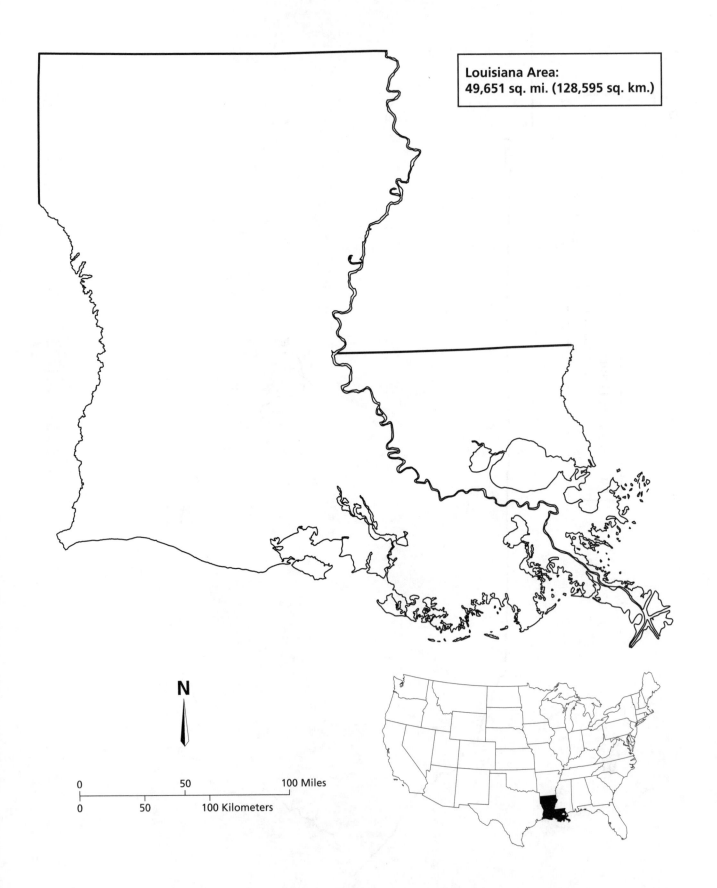

Louisiana Area:
49,651 sq. mi. (128,595 sq. km.)

N

| 0 | | 50 | | 100 Miles |

| 0 | 50 | | 100 Kilometers | |

Maine

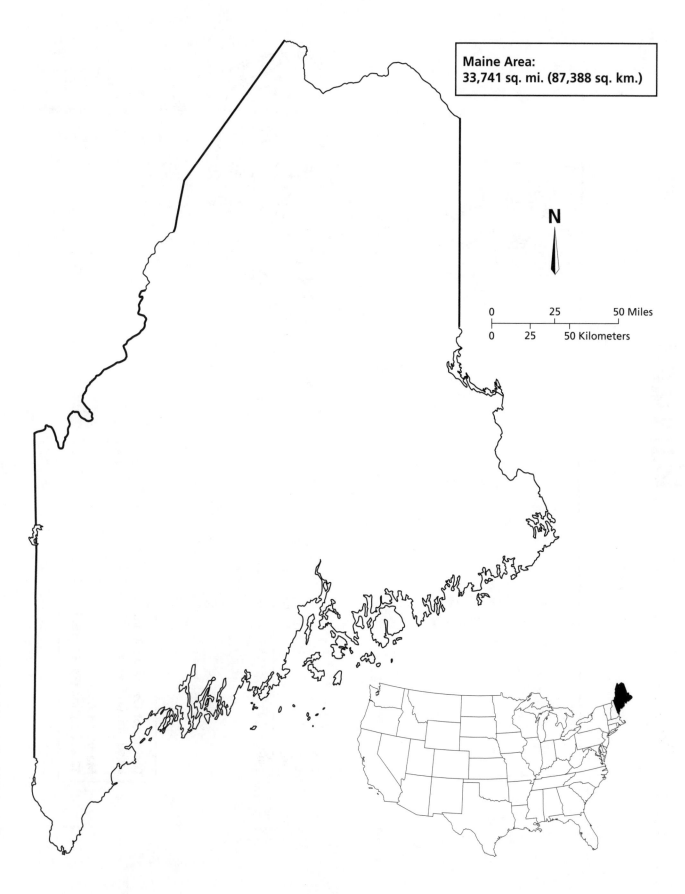

Maine Area:
33,741 sq. mi. (87,388 sq. km.)

N

| 0 | 25 | 50 Miles |

| 0 | 25 | 50 Kilometers |

Maryland

N

0	25	25	50 Miles
0	25		50 Kilometers

District of Columbia Area:
69 sq. mi. (179 sq. km.)

Maryland Area:
12,297 sq. mi. (31,849 sq. km.)

U.S. and World Map Outlines © 2004 Creative Teaching Press

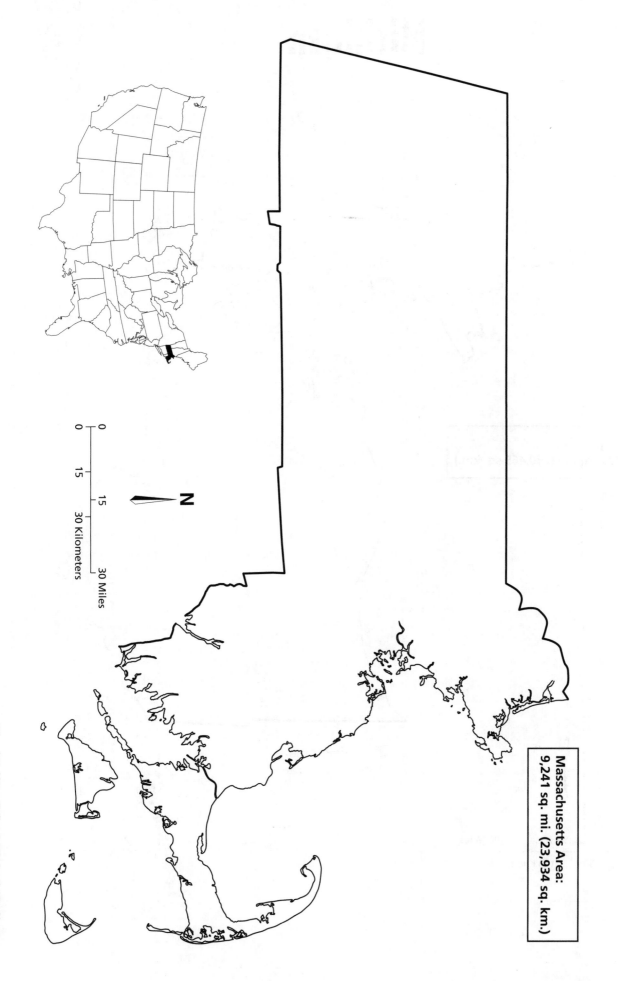

Massachusetts

Massachusetts Area:
9,241 sq. mi. (23,934 sq. km.)

0
0
15
15
15
15
30 Kilometers
30 Miles

N

Michigan

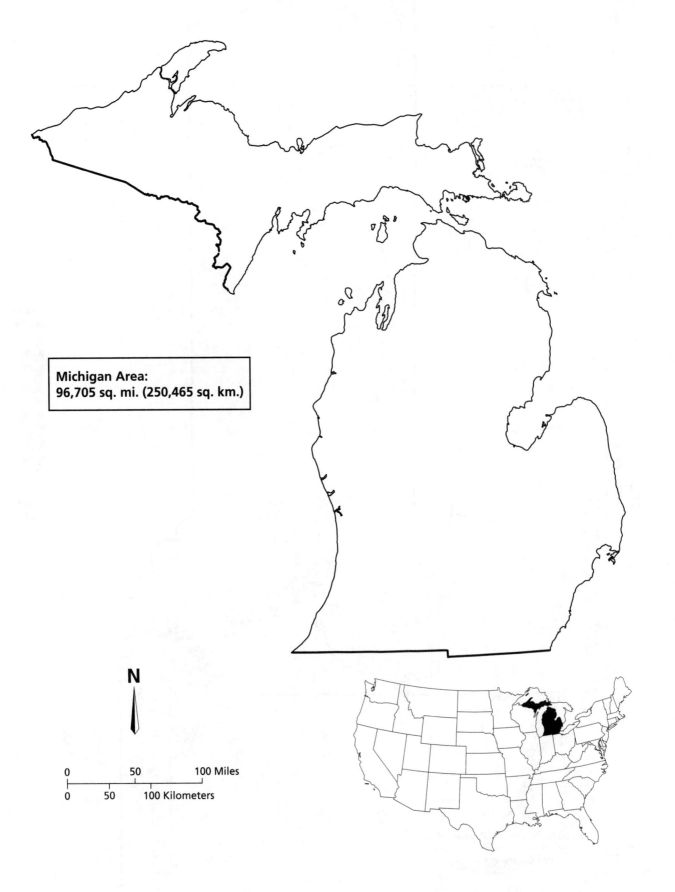

Michigan Area:
96,705 sq. mi. (250,465 sq. km.)

N

| 0 | 50 | 100 Miles |
| 0 | 50 | 100 Kilometers |

Minnesota

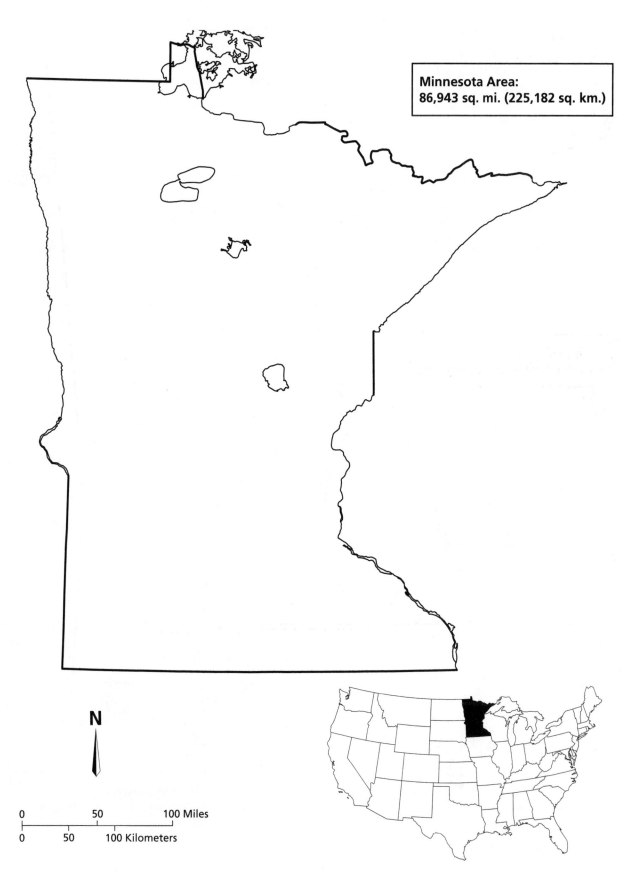

Minnesota Area:
86,943 sq. mi. (225,182 sq. km.)

N

0   50   100 Miles

0   50   100 Kilometers

Mississippi

N

0   25   50 Miles
0   25   50 Kilometers

Mississippi Area:
48,286 sq. mi. (125,060 sq. km.)

Missouri

Missouri Area:
69,709 sq. mi. (180,546 sq. km.)

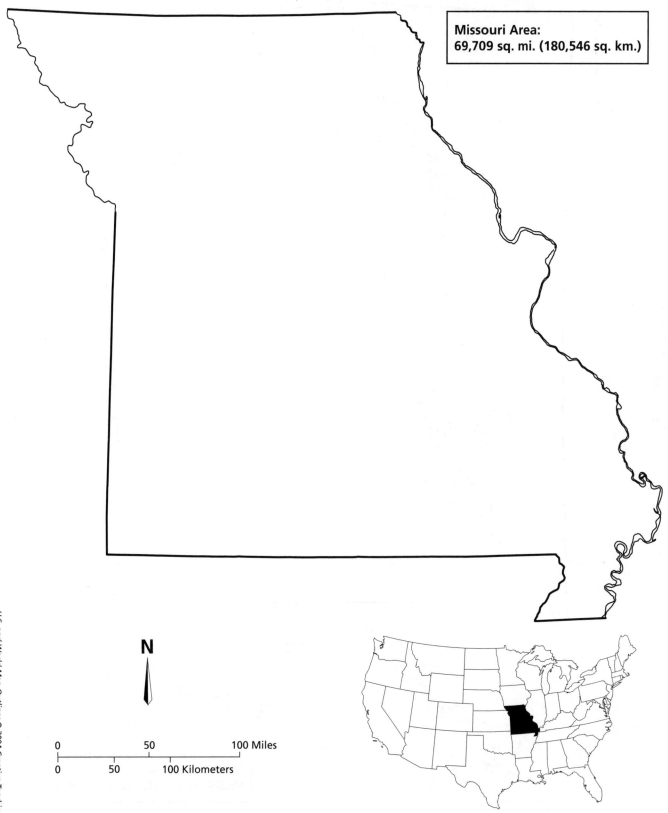

N

0   50   100 Miles

0   50   100 Kilometers

Montana

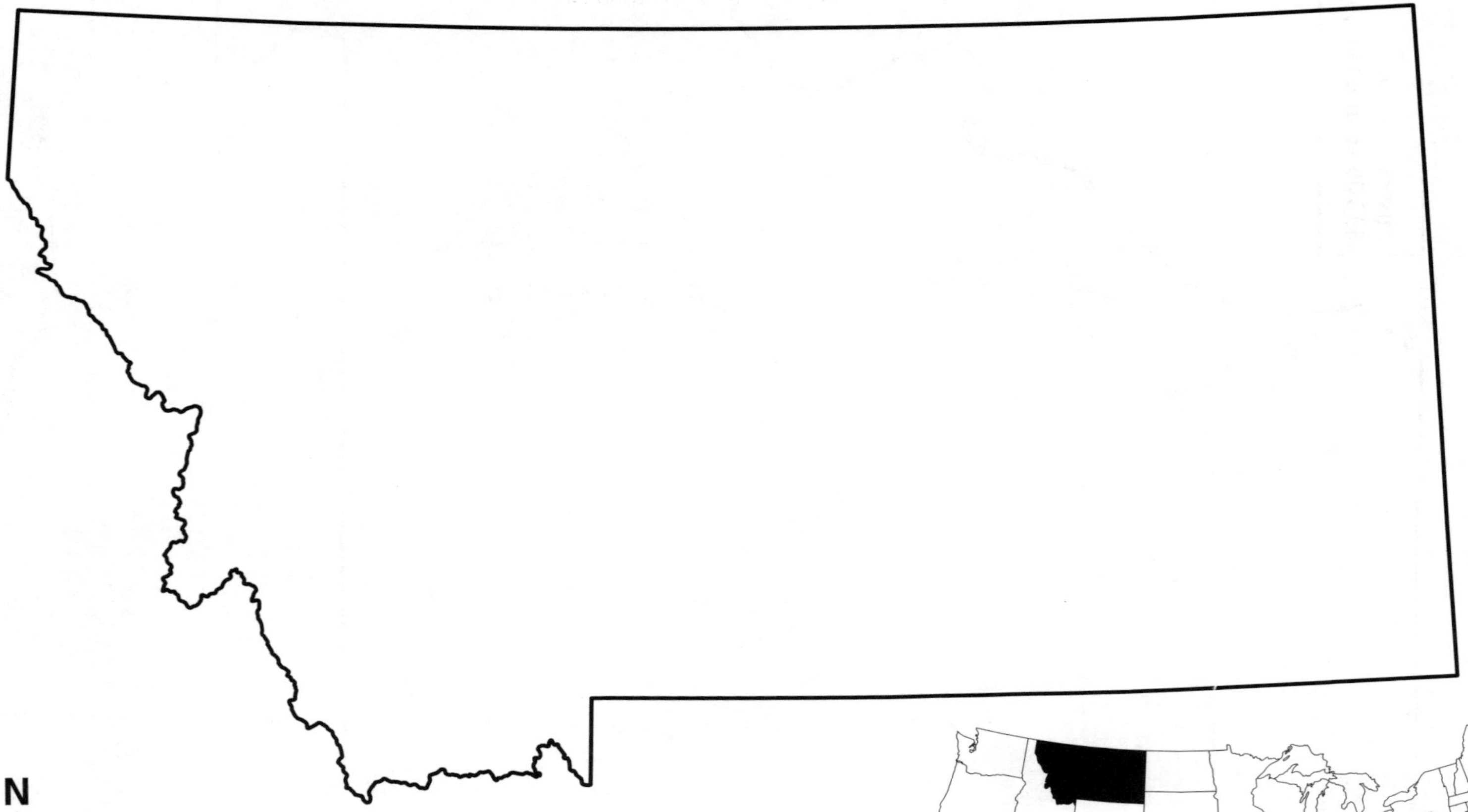

Montana Area:
147,046 sq. mi. (380,849 sq. km.)

100 Miles

100 Kilometers

N

50

50

50

0

0

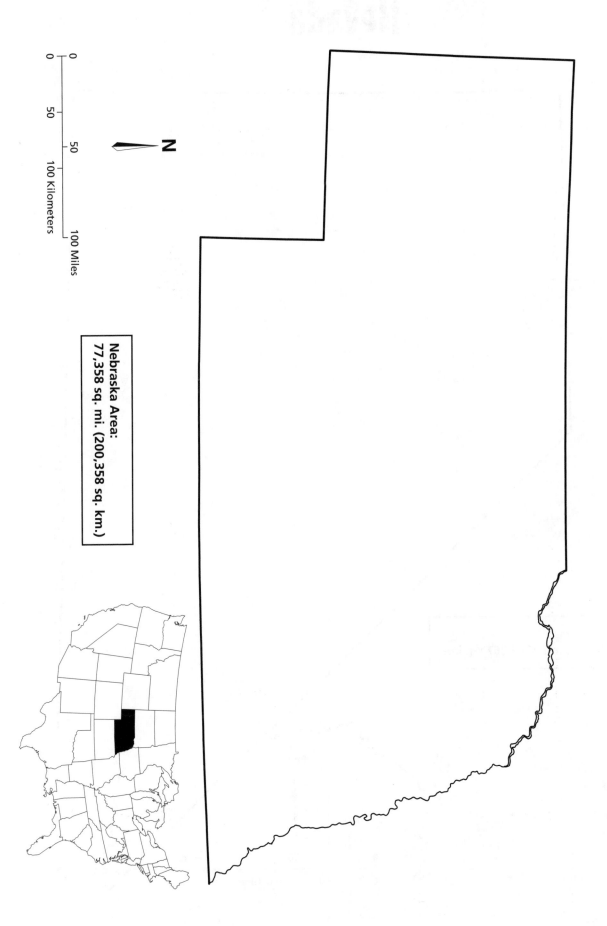

Nebraska

Nebraska Area:
77,358 sq. mi. (200,358 sq. km.)

N

0
0
50
50
100 Kilometers
100 Miles

Nevada

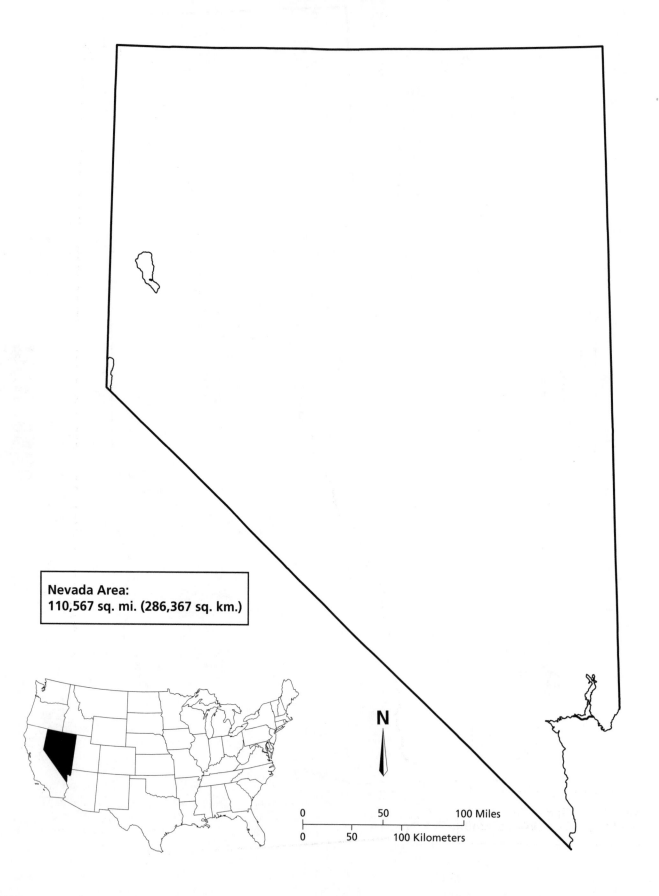

Nevada Area:
110,567 sq. mi. (286,367 sq. km.)

N

| 0 | 50 | 100 Miles |

| 0 | 50 | 100 Kilometers |

New Hampshire

N

0	10	20 Miles
0	10	20 Kilometers

New Hampshire Area:
9,283 sq. mi. (24,044 sq. km.)

New Jersey

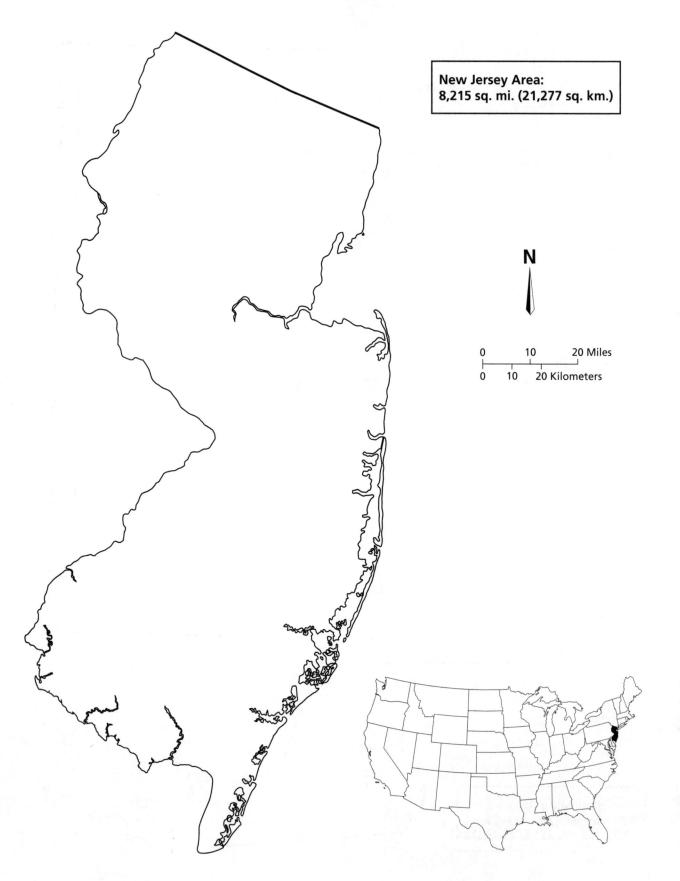

New Jersey Area:
8,215 sq. mi. (21,277 sq. km.)

N

0   10   20 Miles
0   10   20 Kilometers

New Mexico

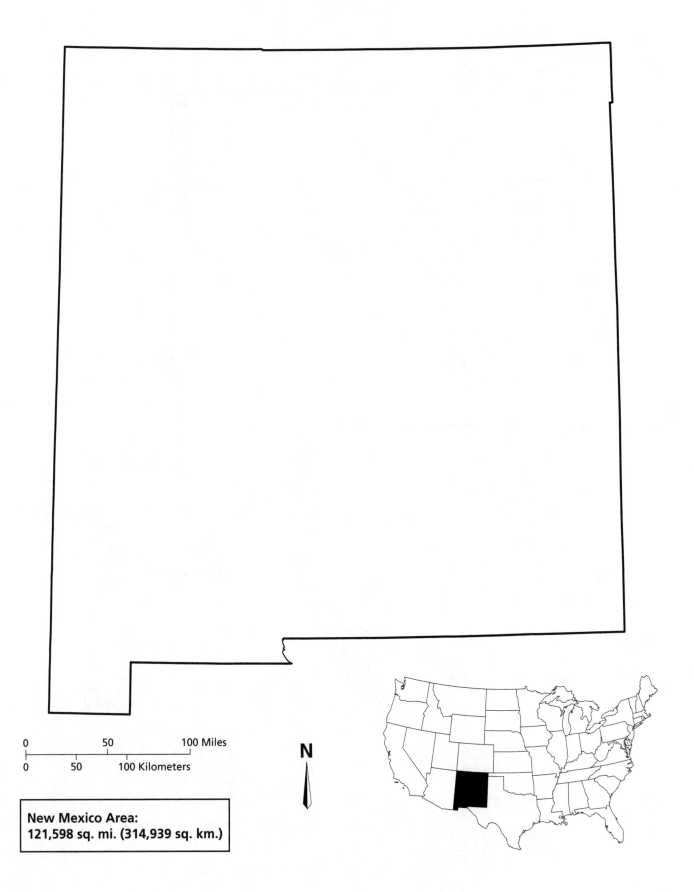

0   50   100 Miles
0   50   100 Kilometers

N

New Mexico Area:
121,598 sq. mi. (314,939 sq. km.)

New York

New York Area:
53,989 sq. mi. (139,833 sq. km.)

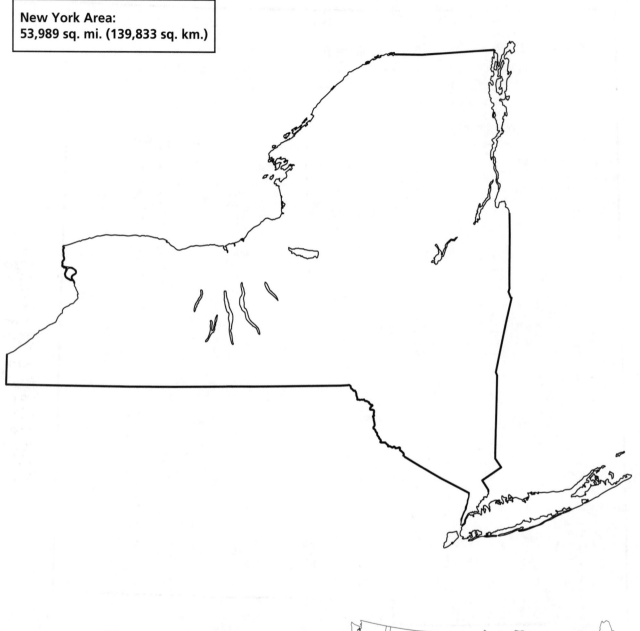

N

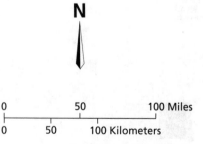

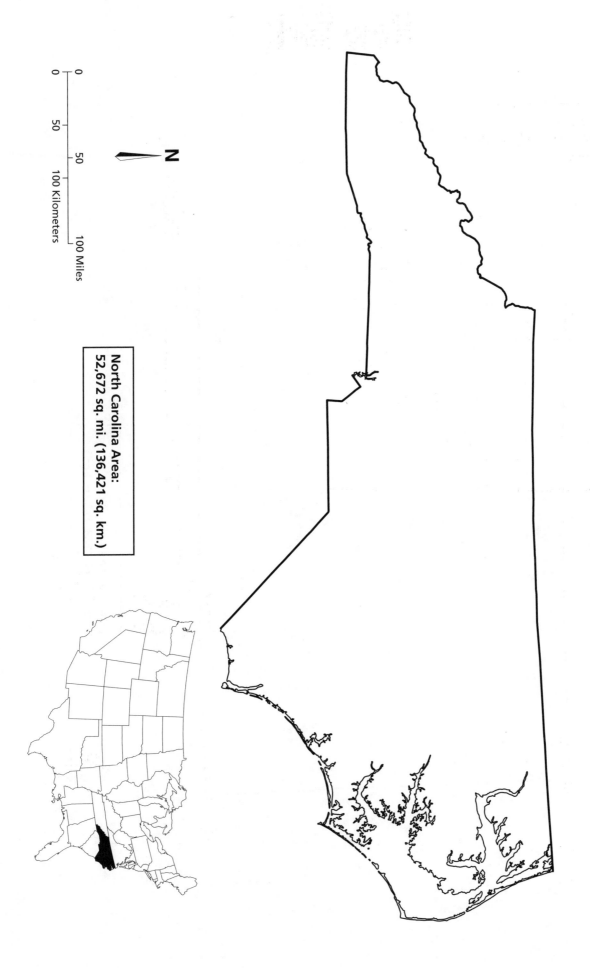

North Carolina

North Carolina Area:
52,672 sq. mi. (136,421 sq. km.)

N

0
0
50
50
100 Kilometers
100 Miles

North Dakota

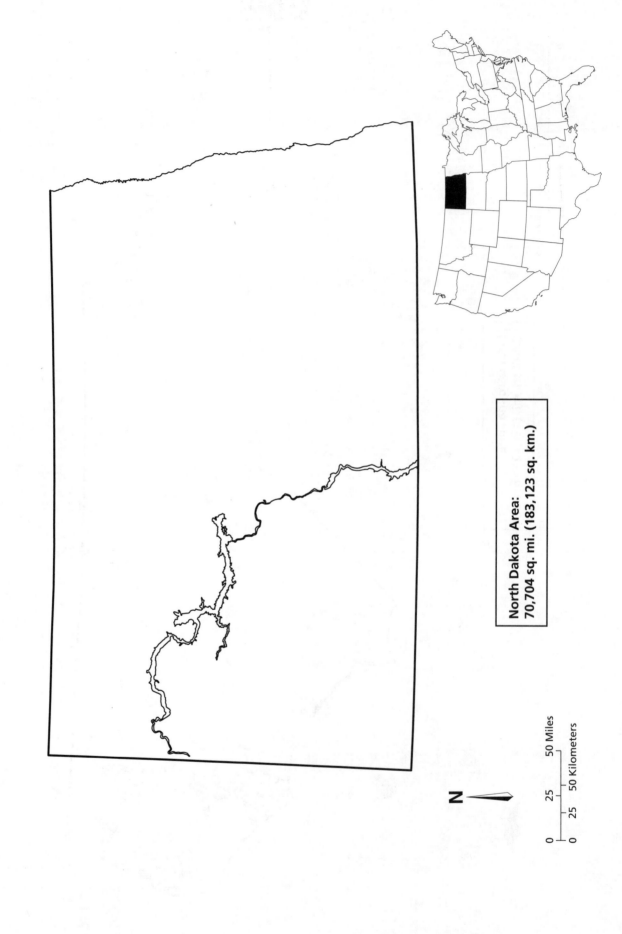

North Dakota Area:
70,704 sq. mi. (183,123 sq. km.)

N

0   25   50 Miles

0   25   50 Kilometers

Ohio

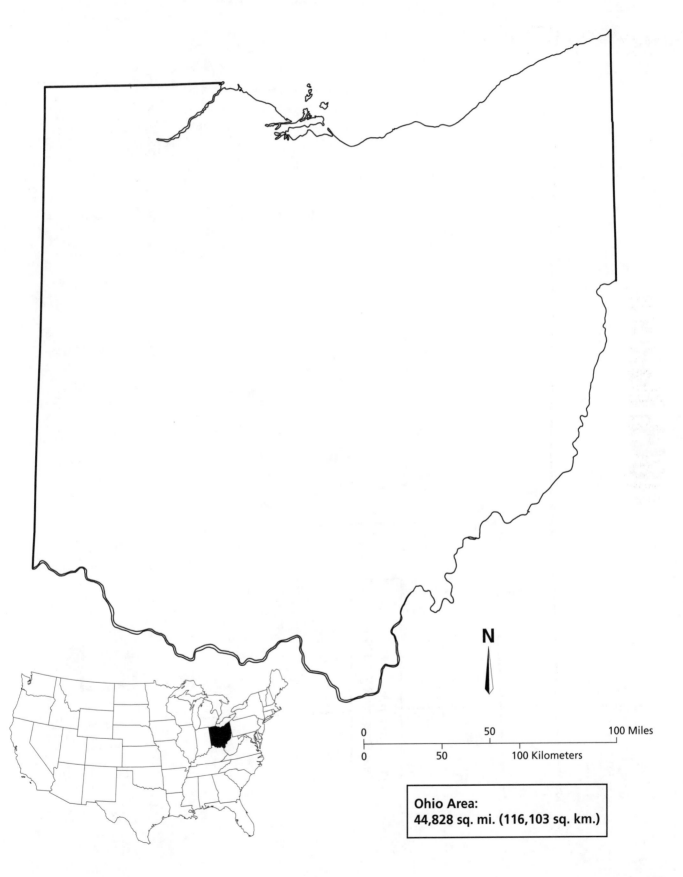

N

0   50   100 Miles
0   50   100 Kilometers

Ohio Area:
44,828 sq. mi. (116,103 sq. km.)

Oklahoma

Oklahoma Area:
69,903 sq. mi. (181,048 sq. km.)

N

0   50   100 Miles

0   50   100 Kilometers

Oregon

Oregon Area:
97,132 sq. mi. (251,571 sq. km.)

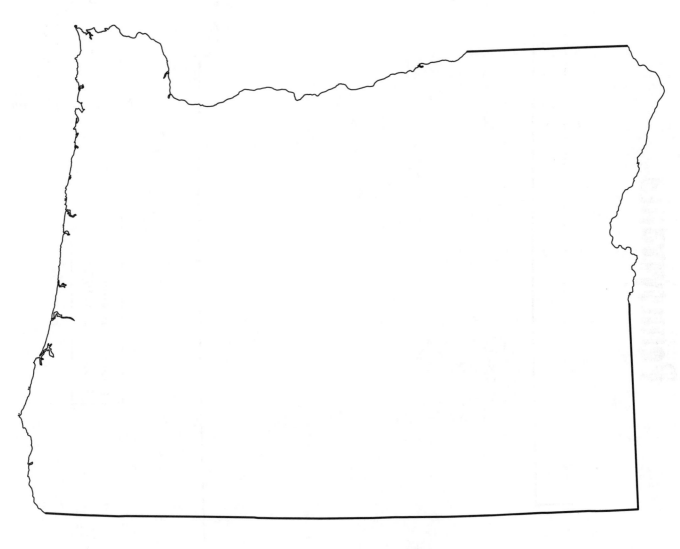

N

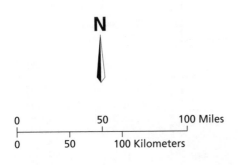

| 0 | | 50 | | 100 Miles |
| 0 | 50 | | 100 Kilometers | |

U.S. and World Map Outlines © 2004 Creative Teaching Press

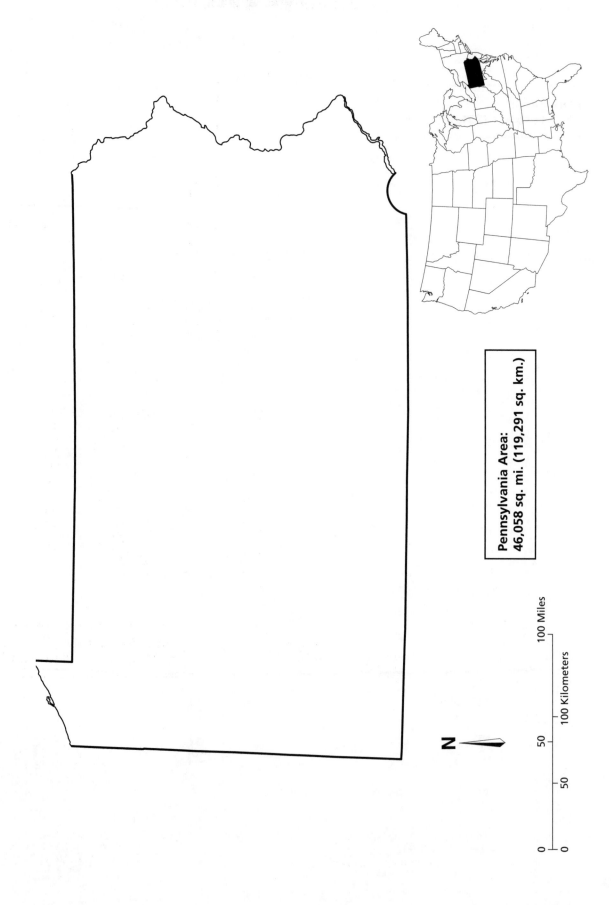

Pennsylvania

Pennsylvania Area:
46,058 sq. mi. (119,291 sq. km.)

N

100 Miles

100 Kilometers

0   50   50   100

0

Rhode Island

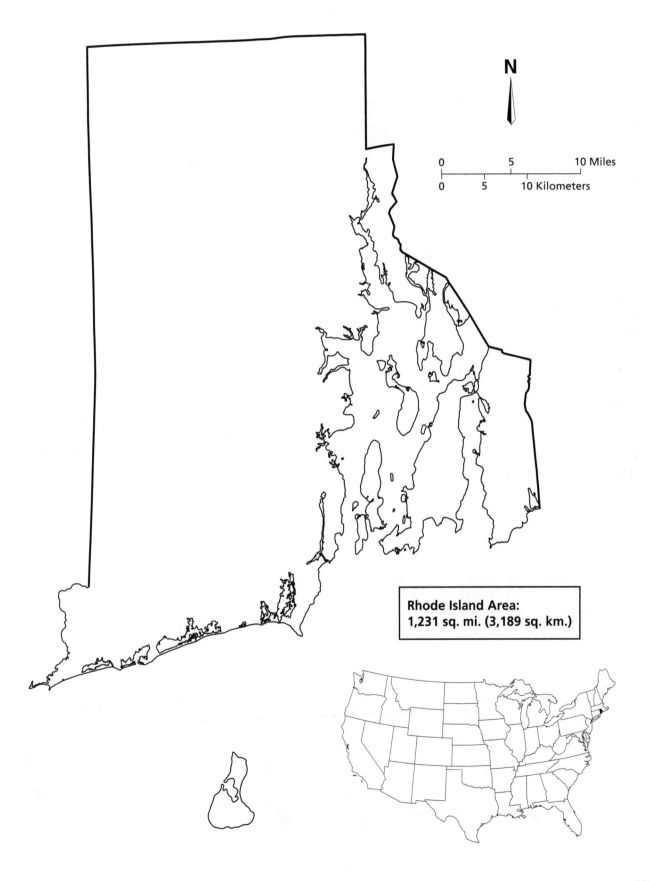

N

| 0 | | 5 | | 10 Miles |

| 0 | 5 | | 10 Kilometers |

Rhode Island Area:
1,231 sq. mi. (3,189 sq. km.)

South Carolina

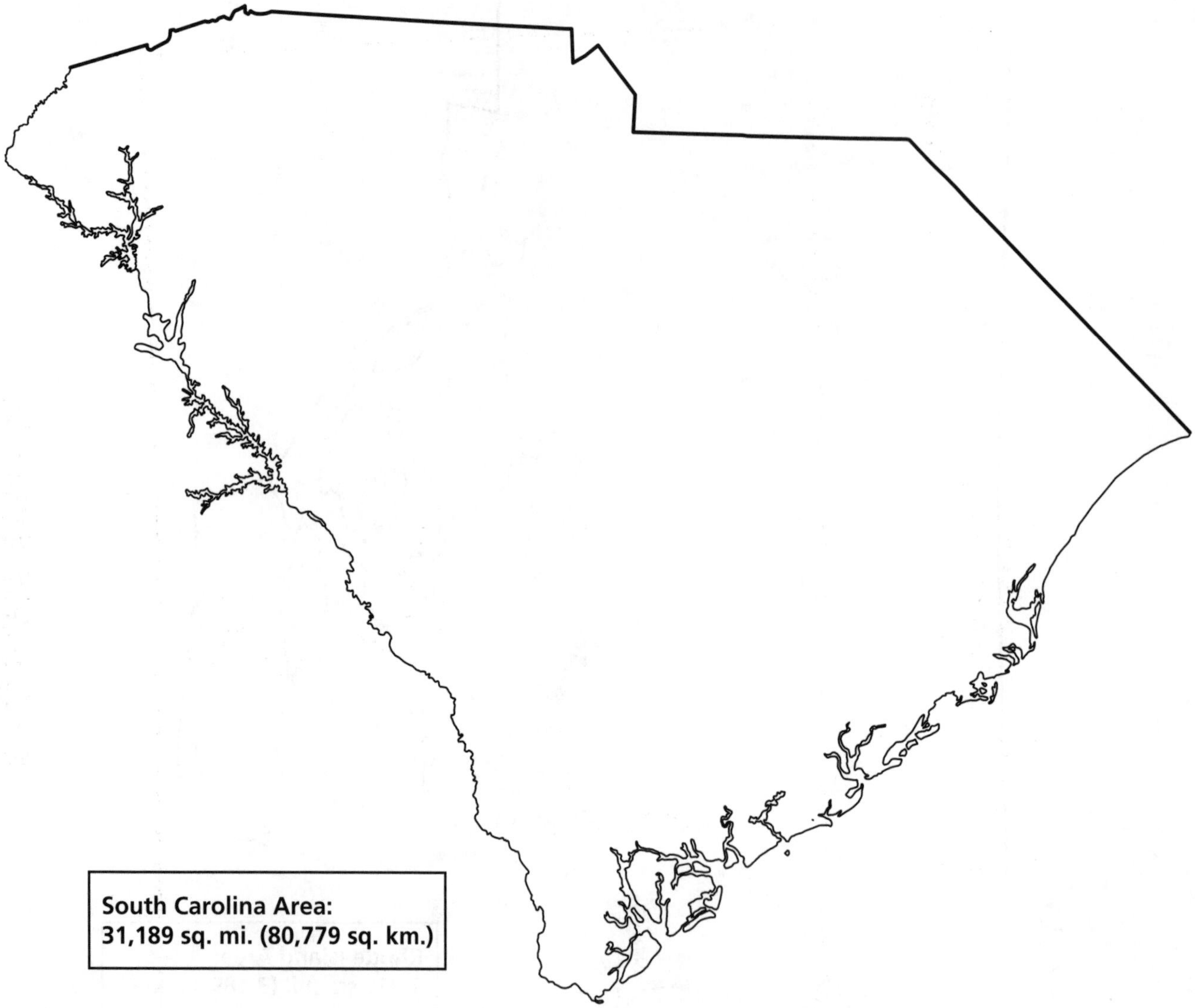

South Carolina Area:
31,189 sq. mi. (80,779 sq. km.)

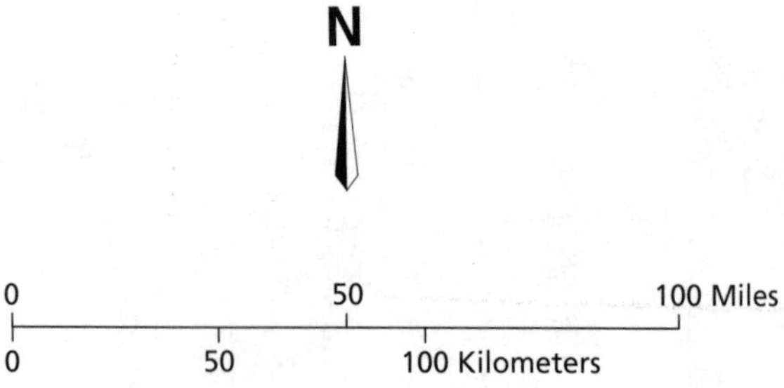

N

0   50   100 Miles

0   50   100 Kilometers

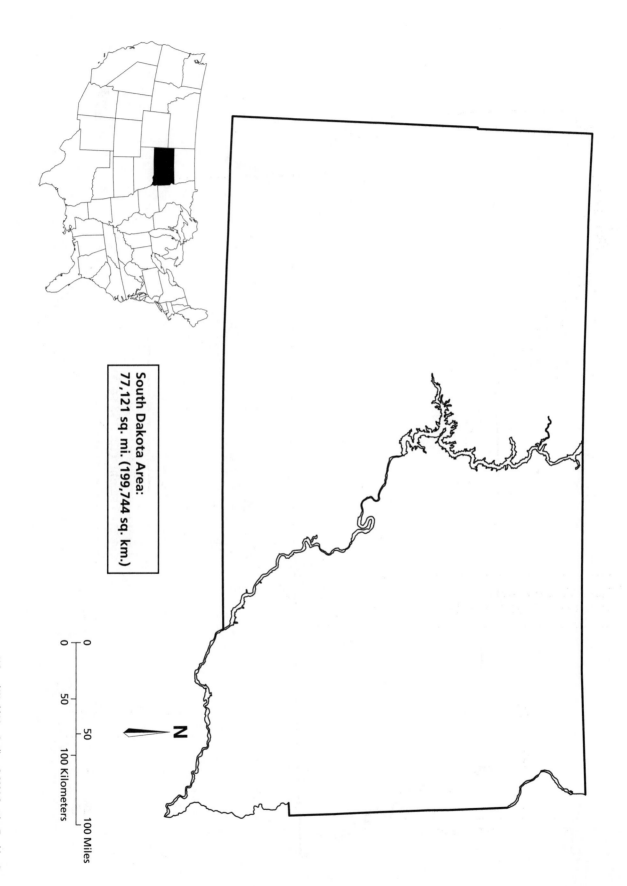

South Dakota

South Dakota Area:
77,121 sq. mi. (199,744 sq. km.)

N

0
0

50

50

100 Kilometers

100 Miles

Tennessee

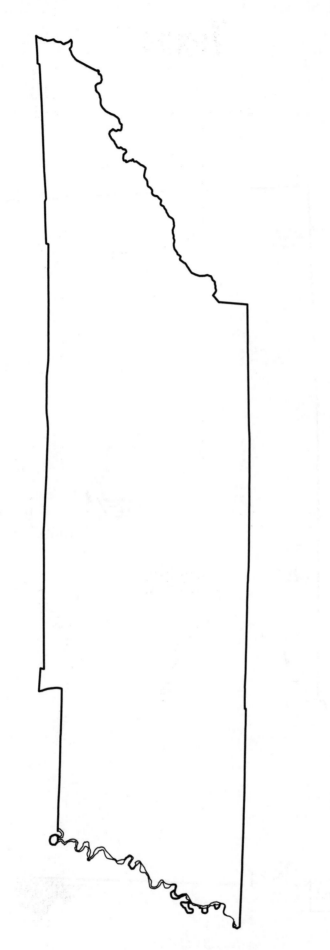

Tennessee Area:
42,146 sq. mi. (109,158 sq. km.)

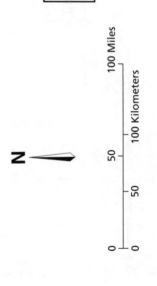

N

| 0 | 50 | 100 Miles |
| 0 | 50 | 100 Kilometers |

Texas

N

0   50   100 Miles
0   50   100 Kilometers

Texas Area:
267,277 sq. mi. (692,248 sq. km.)

Utah

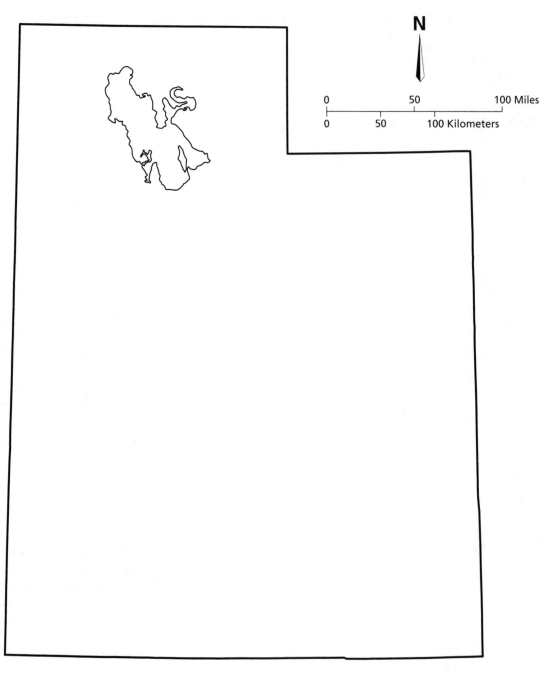

N

| 0 | 50 | 100 Miles |
| 0 | 50 | 100 Kilometers |

Utah Area:
84,904 sq. mi. (219,902 sq. km.)

U.S. and World Map Outlines © 2004 Creative Teaching Press

Vermont

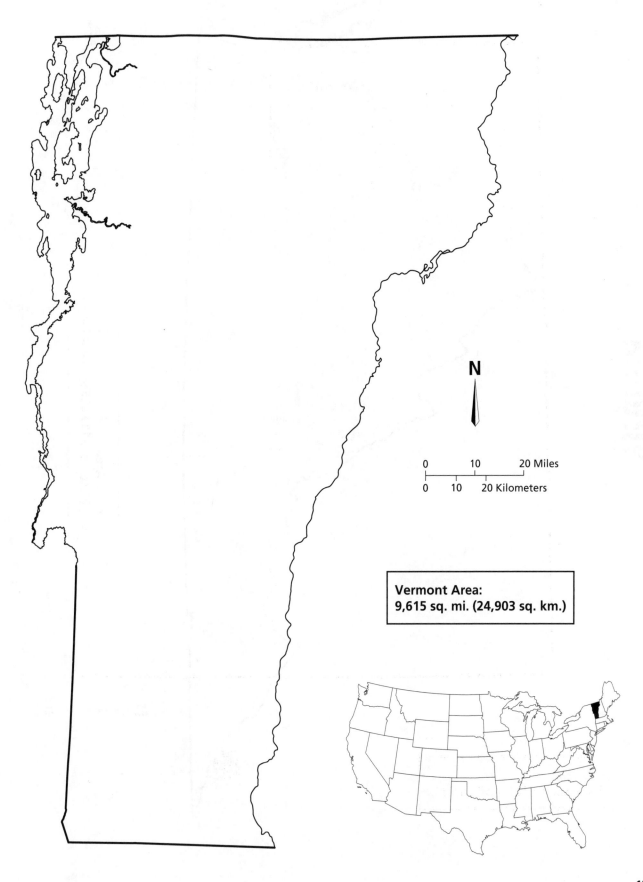

N

| 0 | 10 | 20 Miles |
| 0 | 10 | 20 Kilometers |

Vermont Area:
9,615 sq. mi. (24,903 sq. km.)

Virginia

Virginia Area:
42,326 sq. mi. (109,625 sq. km.)

N

| 0 | 50 | 100 Miles |

| 0 | 50 | 100 Kilometers |

U.S. and World Map Outlines © 2004 Creative Teaching Press

Washington

U.S. and World Map Outlines © 2004 Creative Teaching Press

N

0
0

50

50

100 Kilometers

100 Miles

**Washington Area:
70,637 sq. mi. (182,949 sq. km.)**

West Virginia

N

50   0   50   100 Kilometers

0   50   100 Miles

West Virginia Area:
24,231 sq. mi. (62,759 sq. km.)

U.S. and World Map Outlines © 2004 Creative Teaching Press

Wisconsin

Wisconsin Area:
65,499 sq. mi. (169,643 sq. km.)

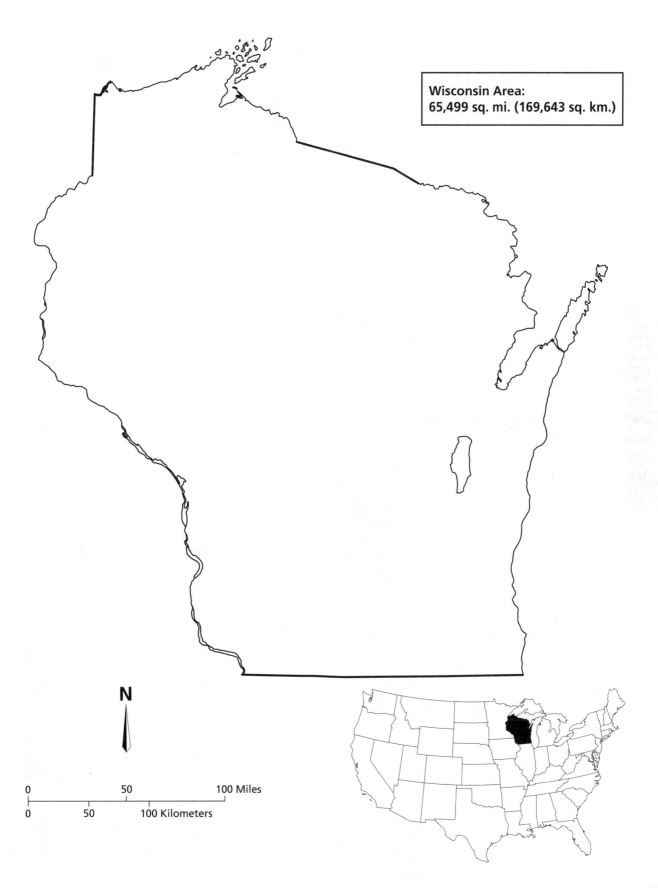

N

| 0 | | 50 | | 100 Miles |
| 0 | 50 | | 100 Kilometers | |

Wyoming

Wyoming Area:
97,818 sq. mi. (253,349 sq. km.)

N

100 Miles

50

100 Kilometers

50

50

0

0